Perception Industries LLC

THE ULTIMATE MLM
90-DAY RUN
WORKBOOK

90-Day Run

Month: _____   Month: _____   Month: _____

SUN	MON	TUE	WED	THU	FRI	SAT

SUN	MON	TUE	WED	THU	FRI	SAT

SUN	MON	TUE	WED	THU	FRI	SAT

Level 2 Downline Rank-Ups	
Level 3 Downline Rank-Ups	
Level 4 Downline Rank-Ups	
Level 5 Downline Rank-Ups	

Average Monthly Sales Income	
Average Monthly Residual Income	
Average Monthly Recruits	
Average Monthly Downline Ranks	

90-Day Run Plan

_____

_____

_____

_____

_____

_____

_____

_____

_____

_____

_____

90-Day Run Notes

_____

_____

_____

_____

_____

_____

_____

_____

_____

_____

_____

_____

_____

_____

_____

_____

_____

_____

_____

MONTH OF: _____

SUNDAY	MONDAY	TUESDAY	WEDNESDAY	THURSDAY	FRIDAY	SATURDAY

Monthly Goals	
Personal Sales	
Team Sales	
Personal Recruits	
Team Recruits	
Monthly Sales Income	
Monthly Residual Income	

Monthly Results	
Personal Sales	
Team Sales	
Personal Recruits	
Team Recruits	
Monthly Sales Income	
Monthly Residual Income	

Month End Review

_____

_____

_____

_____

90-Day Run Notes

WEEKLY ACTIVITY LOG / WEEK OF: _____

Be the Most Productive Person You Can Be At All Times

	SUNDAY	MONDAY	TUESDAY	WEDNESDAY	THURSDAY	FRIDAY	SATURDAY
8am							
9am							
10am							
11am							
12 noon							
1pm							
2pm							
3pm							
4pm							
5pm							
6pm							
7pm							
8pm							
9pm							

Persistence:

"Firm or obstinate continuance in a course of action in spite of difficulty or opposition."

Massive Action Plan To Get $_____ / Yr. Income

Weekly Activity Planner For The Week Of: _____

WEEKLY	GOAL	SUN	MON	TUE	WED	THU	FRI	SAT
PROSPECTS	20							
CALLS	100							
INTERVIEWS	15							
INVITES	10							
MEETINGS	10							
SIGN UPS								
SALES	$							
RESIDUALS	$							

MTD #'s	RECRUITS	RESIDUALS	SALES
PERSONAL			
TEAM			

PROSPECTS
1
2
3
4
5
6
7
8

MEETINGS
1
2
3
4
5
6
7
8
9
10

CALLS
1
2
3
4
5
6
7
8
9
10
11
12
13
14
15

INTERVIEWS
1
2
3
4
5
6
7
8
9
10

DAILY MASSIVE ACTION PLAN

Goals & Affirmations For Day		Time:		Date:	

DAILY SCHEDULE	PEOPLE TO CONTACT	THINGS TO DO
6:00am		
7:00am		
8:00am		
9:00am		
10:00am		
11:00am		
12:00 Noon		
1:00pm		
2:00pm		
3:00pm		
4:00pm		

	ACTION TAKEN	GOAL	RESULT
5:00pm	PROSPECTS	3-10	
6:00pm	CALLS	20-30	
	INTERVIEWS	1-4	
9:00pm	INVITES	2-5	
	MEETINGS	2-3	

	RESULTS CATEGORY	RESULTS	
10:00pm	RECRUITS		
11:00pm	SALES		
	RESIDUALS		

PROSPECT GENERATION SHEET

M = Married   C = Children   H = Home Owner   FT = Full-Time Job

NAME	PHONE	NOTES (CIRCLE APPLICABLE)	
1			M C H FT
2			M C H FT
3			M C H FT
4			M C H FT
5			M C H FT
6			M C H FT
7			M C H FT
8			M C H FT
9			M C H FT
10			M C H FT

PROSPECT GENERATION SHEET

M = Married   C = Children   H = Home Owner   FT = Full-Time Job

NAME	PHONE	NOTES (CIRCLE APPLICABLE)	
1			M C H FT
2			M C H FT
3			M C H FT
4			M C H FT
5			M C H FT
6			M C H FT
7			M C H FT
8			M C H FT
9			M C H FT
10			M C H FT

FOLLOW UP SHEET

NAME	PHONE	NOTES

DAILY MASSIVE ACTION PLAN

Goals & Affirmations For Day	Time:	Date:	

DAILY SCHEDULE	PEOPLE TO CONTACT	THINGS TO DO
6:00am		
7:00am		
8:00am		
9:00am		
10:00am		
11:00am		
12:00 Noon		
1:00pm		
2:00pm		
3:00pm		
4:00pm		

	ACTION TAKEN	GOAL	RESULT
5:00pm	PROSPECTS	3-10	
6:00pm	CALLS	20-30	
	INTERVIEWS	1-4	
9:00pm	INVITES	2-5	
	MEETINGS	2-3	

	RESULTS CATEGORY	RESULTS
10:00pm	RECRUITS	
11:00pm	SALES	
	RESIDUALS	

PROSPECT GENERATION SHEET

M = Married   C = Children   H = Home Owner   FT = Full-Time Job

NAME	PHONE	NOTES (CIRCLE APPLICABLE)
1		M C H FT
2		M C H FT
3		M C H FT
4		M C H FT
5		M C H FT
6		M C H FT
7		M C H FT
8		M C H FT
9		M C H FT
10		M C H FT

PROSPECT GENERATION SHEET

M = Married   C = Children   H = Home Owner   FT = Full-Time Job

NAME	PHONE	NOTES (CIRCLE APPLICABLE)
1		M C H FT
2		M C H FT
3		M C H FT
4		M C H FT
5		M C H FT
6		M C H FT
7		M C H FT
8		M C H FT
9		M C H FT
10		M C H FT

FOLLOW UP SHEET

NAME	PHONE	NOTES

DAILY MASSIVE ACTION PLAN

Goals & Affirmations For Day	Time:	Date:

DAILY SCHEDULE	PEOPLE TO CONTACT	THINGS TO DO
6:00am		
7:00am		
8:00am		
9:00am		
10:00am		
11:00am		
12:00 Noon		
1:00pm		
2:00pm		
3:00pm		
4:00pm		

DAILY SCHEDULE	ACTION TAKEN	GOAL	RESULT
5:00pm	PROSPECTS	3-10	
	CALLS	20-30	
6:00pm	INTERVIEWS	1-4	
	INVITES	2-5	
9:00pm	MEETINGS	2-3	
10:00pm	RESULTS CATEGORY	RESULTS	
	RECRUITS		
11:00pm	SALES		
	RESIDUALS		

PROSPECT GENERATION SHEET

M = Married   C = Children   H = Home Owner   FT = Full-Time Job

NAME	PHONE	NOTES (CIRCLE APPLICABLE)
1		M C H FT
2		M C H FT
3		M C H FT
4		M C H FT
5		M C H FT
6		M C H FT
7		M C H FT
8		M C H FT
9		M C H FT
10		M C H FT

PROSPECT GENERATION SHEET

M = Married   C = Children   H = Home Owner   FT = Full-Time Job

NAME	PHONE	NOTES (CIRCLE APPLICABLE)
1		M C H FT
2		M C H FT
3		M C H FT
4		M C H FT
5		M C H FT
6		M C H FT
7		M C H FT
8		M C H FT
9		M C H FT
10		M C H FT

FOLLOW UP SHEET

NAME	PHONE	NOTES

DAILY MASSIVE ACTION PLAN

Goals & Affirmations For Day	Time:	Date:

DAILY SCHEDULE	PEOPLE TO CONTACT	THINGS TO DO
6:00am		
7:00am		
8:00am		
9:00am		
10:00am		
11:00am		
12:00 Noon		
1:00pm		
2:00pm		
3:00pm		
4:00pm		

	ACTION TAKEN	GOAL	RESULT
5:00pm	PROSPECTS	3-10	
6:00pm	CALLS	20-30	
	INTERVIEWS	1-4	
9:00pm	INVITES	2-5	
	MEETINGS	2-3	

	RESULTS CATEGORY	RESULTS
10:00pm	RECRUITS	
11:00pm	SALES	
	RESIDUALS	

PROSPECT GENERATION SHEET

M = Married   C = Children   H = Home Owner   FT = Full-Time Job

NAME	PHONE	NOTES (CIRCLE APPLICABLE)
1		M C H FT
2		M C H FT
3		M C H FT
4		M C H FT
5		M C H FT
6		M C H FT
7		M C H FT
8		M C H FT
9		M C H FT
10		M C H FT

PROSPECT GENERATION SHEET

M = Married   C = Children   H = Home Owner   FT = Full-Time Job

NAME	PHONE	NOTES (CIRCLE APPLICABLE)
1		M C H FT
2		M C H FT
3		M C H FT
4		M C H FT
5		M C H FT
6		M C H FT
7		M C H FT
8		M C H FT
9		M C H FT
10		M C H FT

FOLLOW UP SHEET

NAME	PHONE	NOTES

DAILY MASSIVE ACTION PLAN

Goals & Affirmations For Day	Time:	Date:

DAILY SCHEDULE	PEOPLE TO CONTACT	THINGS TO DO
6:00am		
7:00am		
8:00am		
9:00am		
10:00am		
11:00am		
12:00 Noon		
1:00pm		
2:00pm		
3:00pm		
4:00pm		

DAILY SCHEDULE	ACTION TAKEN	GOAL	RESULT
5:00pm	PROSPECTS	3-10	
6:00pm	CALLS	20-30	
	INTERVIEWS	1-4	
9:00pm	INVITES	2-5	
	MEETINGS	2-3	

	RESULTS CATEGORY	RESULTS	
10:00pm	RECRUITS		
11:00pm	SALES		
	RESIDUALS		

PROSPECT GENERATION SHEET

M = Married   C = Children   H = Home Owner   FT = Full-Time Job

NAME	PHONE	NOTES (CIRCLE APPLICABLE)
1		M C H FT
2		M C H FT
3		M C H FT
4		M C H FT
5		M C H FT
6		M C H FT
7		M C H FT
8		M C H FT
9		M C H FT
10		M C H FT

PROSPECT GENERATION SHEET

M = Married   C = Children   H = Home Owner   FT = Full-Time Job

NAME	PHONE	NOTES (CIRCLE APPLICABLE)
1		M C H FT
2		M C H FT
3		M C H FT
4		M C H FT
5		M C H FT
6		M C H FT
7		M C H FT
8		M C H FT
9		M C H FT
10		M C H FT

FOLLOW UP SHEET

NAME	PHONE	NOTES

DAILY MASSIVE ACTION PLAN

Goals & Affirmations For Day	Time:	Date:

DAILY SCHEDULE	PEOPLE TO CONTACT	THINGS TO DO
6:00am		
7:00am		
8:00am		
9:00am		
10:00am		
11:00am		
12:00 Noon		
1:00pm		
2:00pm		
3:00pm		
4:00pm		

	ACTION TAKEN	GOAL	RESULT
5:00pm	PROSPECTS	3-10	
6:00pm	CALLS	20-30	
	INTERVIEWS	1-4	
9:00pm	INVITES	2-5	
	MEETINGS	2-3	

	RESULTS CATEGORY	RESULTS
10:00pm	RECRUITS	
11:00pm	SALES	
	RESIDUALS	

PROSPECT GENERATION SHEET

M = Married   C = Children   H = Home Owner   FT = Full-Time Job

NAME	PHONE	NOTES (CIRCLE APPLICABLE)	
1			M C H FT
2			M C H FT
3			M C H FT
4			M C H FT
5			M C H FT
6			M C H FT
7			M C H FT
8			M C H FT
9			M C H FT
10			M C H FT

PROSPECT GENERATION SHEET

M = Married   C = Children   H = Home Owner   FT = Full-Time Job

NAME	PHONE	NOTES (CIRCLE APPLICABLE)
1		M C H FT
2		M C H FT
3		M C H FT
4		M C H FT
5		M C H FT
6		M C H FT
7		M C H FT
8		M C H FT
9		M C H FT
10		M C H FT

FOLLOW UP SHEET

NAME	PHONE	NOTES

DAILY MASSIVE ACTION PLAN

Goals & Affirmations For Day	Time:	Date:

DAILY SCHEDULE	PEOPLE TO CONTACT	THINGS TO DO
6:00am		
7:00am		
8:00am		
9:00am		
10:00am		
11:00am		
12:00 Noon		
1:00pm		
2:00pm		
3:00pm		
4:00pm		

DAILY SCHEDULE	ACTION TAKEN	GOAL	RESULT
5:00pm	PROSPECTS	3-10	
	CALLS	20-30	
6:00pm	INTERVIEWS	1-4	
	INVITES	2-5	
9:00pm	MEETINGS	2-3	

	RESULTS CATEGORY	RESULTS	
10:00pm	RECRUITS		
11:00pm	SALES		
	RESIDUALS		

PROSPECT GENERATION SHEET

M = Married   C = Children   H = Home Owner   FT = Full-Time Job

NAME	PHONE	NOTES (CIRCLE APPLICABLE)
1		M C H FT
2		M C H FT
3		M C H FT
4		M C H FT
5		M C H FT
6		M C H FT
7		M C H FT
8		M C H FT
9		M C H FT
10		M C H FT

PROSPECT GENERATION SHEET

M = Married   C = Children   H = Home Owner   FT = Full-Time Job

NAME	PHONE	NOTES (CIRCLE APPLICABLE)
1		M C H FT
2		M C H FT
3		M C H FT
4		M C H FT
5		M C H FT
6		M C H FT
7		M C H FT
8		M C H FT
9		M C H FT
10		M C H FT

FOLLOW UP SHEET

NAME	PHONE	NOTES

WEEKLY ACTIVITY LOG / WEEK OF: _____

Be the Most Productive Person You Can Be At All Times

	SUNDAY	MONDAY	TUESDAY	WEDNESDAY	THURSDAY	FRIDAY	SATURDAY
8am							
9am							
10am							
11am							
12 noon							
1pm							
2pm							
3pm							
4pm							
5pm							
6pm							
7pm							
8pm							
9pm							

Persistence:

"Firm or obstinate continuance in a course of action in spite of difficulty or opposition."

Massive Action Plan To Get $_____ / Yr. Income

Weekly Activity Planner For The Week Of: _____

WEEKLY	GOAL	SUN	MON	TUE	WED	THU	FRI	SAT
PROSPECTS	20							
CALLS	100							
INTERVIEWS	15							
INVITES	10							
MEETINGS	10							
SIGN UPS								
SALES	$							
RESIDUALS	$							

MTD #'s	RECRUITS	RESIDUALS	SALES
PERSONAL			
TEAM			

PROSPECTS
1
2
3
4
5
6
7
8

MEETINGS
1
2
3
4
5
6
7
8
9
10

CALLS
1
2
3
4
5
6
7
8
9
10
11
12
13
14
15

INTERVIEWS
1
2
3
4
5
6
7
8
9
10

DAILY MASSIVE ACTION PLAN

Goals & Affirmations For Day	Time:	Date:

DAILY SCHEDULE	PEOPLE TO CONTACT	THINGS TO DO
6:00am		
7:00am		
8:00am		
9:00am		
10:00am		
11:00am		
12:00 Noon		
1:00pm		
2:00pm		
3:00pm		
4:00pm		

DAILY SCHEDULE	ACTION TAKEN	GOAL	RESULT
5:00pm	PROSPECTS	3-10	
6:00pm	CALLS	20-30	
	INTERVIEWS	1-4	
9:00pm	INVITES	2-5	
	MEETINGS	2-3	
10:00pm	RESULTS CATEGORY	RESULTS	
	RECRUITS		
11:00pm	SALES		
	RESIDUALS		

PROSPECT GENERATION SHEET

M = Married   C = Children   H = Home Owner   FT = Full-Time Job

NAME	PHONE	NOTES (CIRCLE APPLICABLE)
1		M C H FT
2		M C H FT
3		M C H FT
4		M C H FT
5		M C H FT
6		M C H FT
7		M C H FT
8		M C H FT
9		M C H FT
10		M C H FT

PROSPECT GENERATION SHEET

M = Married   C = Children   H = Home Owner   FT = Full-Time Job

NAME	PHONE	NOTES (CIRCLE APPLICABLE)
1		M C H FT
2		M C H FT
3		M C H FT
4		M C H FT
5		M C H FT
6		M C H FT
7		M C H FT
8		M C H FT
9		M C H FT
10		M C H FT

FOLLOW UP SHEET

NAME	PHONE	NOTES

DAILY MASSIVE ACTION PLAN

Goals & Affirmations For Day	Time:	Date:

DAILY SCHEDULE	PEOPLE TO CONTACT	THINGS TO DO
6:00am		
7:00am		
8:00am		
9:00am		
10:00am		
11:00am		
12:00 Noon		
1:00pm		
2:00pm		
3:00pm		
4:00pm		

DAILY SCHEDULE	ACTION TAKEN	GOAL	RESULT
5:00pm	PROSPECTS	3-10	
6:00pm	CALLS	20-30	
	INTERVIEWS	1-4	
9:00pm	INVITES	2-5	
	MEETINGS	2-3	
10:00pm	RESULTS CATEGORY	RESULTS	
	RECRUITS		
11:00pm	SALES		
	RESIDUALS		

PROSPECT GENERATION SHEET

M = Married   C = Children   H = Home Owner   FT = Full-Time Job

NAME	PHONE	NOTES (CIRCLE APPLICABLE)
1		M C H FT
2		M C H FT
3		M C H FT
4		M C H FT
5		M C H FT
6		M C H FT
7		M C H FT
8		M C H FT
9		M C H FT
10		M C H FT

PROSPECT GENERATION SHEET

M = Married   C = Children   H = Home Owner   FT = Full-Time Job

NAME	PHONE	NOTES (CIRCLE APPLICABLE)
1		M C H FT
2		M C H FT
3		M C H FT
4		M C H FT
5		M C H FT
6		M C H FT
7		M C H FT
8		M C H FT
9		M C H FT
10		M C H FT

FOLLOW UP SHEET

NAME	PHONE	NOTES

DAILY MASSIVE ACTION PLAN

Goals & Affirmations For Day	Time:		Date:	

DAILY SCHEDULE	PEOPLE TO CONTACT	THINGS TO DO
6:00am		
7:00am		
8:00am		
9:00am		
10:00am		
11:00am		
12:00 Noon		
1:00pm		
2:00pm		
3:00pm		
4:00pm		

DAILY SCHEDULE	ACTION TAKEN	GOAL	RESULT
5:00pm	PROSPECTS	3-10	
	CALLS	20-30	
6:00pm	INTERVIEWS	1-4	
	INVITES	2-5	
9:00pm	MEETINGS	2-3	
	RESULTS CATEGORY	**RESULTS**	
10:00pm	RECRUITS		
	SALES		
11:00pm	RESIDUALS		

PROSPECT GENERATION SHEET

M = Married   C = Children   H = Home Owner   FT = Full-Time Job

NAME	PHONE	NOTES (CIRCLE APPLICABLE)
1		M C H FT
2		M C H FT
3		M C H FT
4		M C H FT
5		M C H FT
6		M C H FT
7		M C H FT
8		M C H FT
9		M C H FT
10		M C H FT

PROSPECT GENERATION SHEET

M = Married   C = Children   H = Home Owner   FT = Full-Time Job

NAME	PHONE	NOTES (CIRCLE APPLICABLE)
1		M C H FT
2		M C H FT
3		M C H FT
4		M C H FT
5		M C H FT
6		M C H FT
7		M C H FT
8		M C H FT
9		M C H FT
10		M C H FT

FOLLOW UP SHEET

NAME	PHONE	NOTES

DAILY MASSIVE ACTION PLAN

Goals & Affirmations For Day	Time:		Date:	

DAILY SCHEDULE	PEOPLE TO CONTACT	THINGS TO DO
6:00am		
7:00am		
8:00am		
9:00am		
10:00am		
11:00am		
12:00 Noon		
1:00pm		
2:00pm		
3:00pm		
4:00pm		

DAILY SCHEDULE	ACTION TAKEN	GOAL	RESULT
5:00pm	PROSPECTS	3-10	
6:00pm	CALLS	20-30	
	INTERVIEWS	1-4	
9:00pm	INVITES	2-5	
	MEETINGS	2-3	
10:00pm	RESULTS CATEGORY	RESULTS	
	RECRUITS		
11:00pm	SALES		
	RESIDUALS		

PROSPECT GENERATION SHEET

M = Married   C = Children   H = Home Owner   FT = Full-Time Job

NAME	PHONE	NOTES (CIRCLE APPLICABLE)	
1			M C H FT
2			M C H FT
3			M C H FT
4			M C H FT
5			M C H FT
6			M C H FT
7			M C H FT
8			M C H FT
9			M C H FT
10			M C H FT

PROSPECT GENERATION SHEET

M = Married   C = Children   H = Home Owner   FT = Full-Time Job

NAME	PHONE	NOTES (CIRCLE APPLICABLE)
1		M C H FT
2		M C H FT
3		M C H FT
4		M C H FT
5		M C H FT
6		M C H FT
7		M C H FT
8		M C H FT
9		M C H FT
10		M C H FT

FOLLOW UP SHEET

NAME	PHONE	NOTES

DAILY MASSIVE ACTION PLAN

Goals & Affirmations For Day	Time:	Date:

DAILY SCHEDULE	PEOPLE TO CONTACT	THINGS TO DO
6:00am		
7:00am		
8:00am		
9:00am		
10:00am		
11:00am		
12:00 Noon		
1:00pm		
2:00pm		
3:00pm		
4:00pm		

DAILY SCHEDULE	ACTION TAKEN	GOAL	RESULT
5:00pm	PROSPECTS	3-10	
6:00pm	CALLS	20-30	
	INTERVIEWS	1-4	
9:00pm	INVITES	2-5	
	MEETINGS	2-3	
10:00pm	RESULTS CATEGORY	RESULTS	
	RECRUITS		
11:00pm	SALES		
	RESIDUALS		

PROSPECT GENERATION SHEET

M = Married   C = Children   H = Home Owner   FT = Full-Time Job

NAME	PHONE	NOTES (CIRCLE APPLICABLE)
1		M C H FT
2		M C H FT
3		M C H FT
4		M C H FT
5		M C H FT
6		M C H FT
7		M C H FT
8		M C H FT
9		M C H FT
10		M C H FT

PROSPECT GENERATION SHEET

M = Married   C = Children   H = Home Owner   FT = Full-Time Job

NAME	PHONE	NOTES (CIRCLE APPLICABLE)
1		M C H FT
2		M C H FT
3		M C H FT
4		M C H FT
5		M C H FT
6		M C H FT
7		M C H FT
8		M C H FT
9		M C H FT
10		M C H FT

FOLLOW UP SHEET

NAME	PHONE	NOTES

DAILY MASSIVE ACTION PLAN

Goals & Affirmations For Day	Time:	Date:

DAILY SCHEDULE	PEOPLE TO CONTACT	THINGS TO DO
6:00am		
7:00am		
8:00am		
9:00am		
10:00am		
11:00am		
12:00 Noon		
1:00pm		
2:00pm		
3:00pm		
4:00pm		

	ACTION TAKEN	GOAL	RESULT
5:00pm	PROSPECTS	3-10	
6:00pm	CALLS	20-30	
	INTERVIEWS	1-4	
9:00pm	INVITES	2-5	
	MEETINGS	2-3	
10:00pm	RESULTS CATEGORY	RESULTS	
	RECRUITS		
11:00pm	SALES		
	RESIDUALS		

PROSPECT GENERATION SHEET

M = Married   C = Children   H = Home Owner   FT = Full-Time Job

NAME	PHONE	NOTES (CIRCLE APPLICABLE)
1		M C H FT
2		M C H FT
3		M C H FT
4		M C H FT
5		M C H FT
6		M C H FT
7		M C H FT
8		M C H FT
9		M C H FT
10		M C H FT

PROSPECT GENERATION SHEET

M = Married   C = Children   H = Home Owner   FT = Full-Time Job

NAME	PHONE	NOTES (CIRCLE APPLICABLE)
1		M C H FT
2		M C H FT
3		M C H FT
4		M C H FT
5		M C H FT
6		M C H FT
7		M C H FT
8		M C H FT
9		M C H FT
10		M C H FT

FOLLOW UP SHEET

NAME	PHONE	NOTES

DAILY MASSIVE ACTION PLAN

Goals & Affirmations For Day	Time:	Date:

DAILY SCHEDULE	PEOPLE TO CONTACT	THINGS TO DO
6:00am		
7:00am		
8:00am		
9:00am		
10:00am		
11:00am		
12:00 Noon		
1:00pm		
2:00pm		
3:00pm		
4:00pm		

DAILY SCHEDULE	ACTION TAKEN	GOAL	RESULT
5:00pm	PROSPECTS	3-10	
6:00pm	CALLS	20-30	
	INTERVIEWS	1-4	
9:00pm	INVITES	2-5	
	MEETINGS	2-3	
10:00pm	RESULTS CATEGORY	RESULTS	
	RECRUITS		
11:00pm	SALES		
	RESIDUALS		

PROSPECT GENERATION SHEET

M = Married   C = Children   H = Home Owner   FT = Full-Time Job

NAME	PHONE	NOTES (CIRCLE APPLICABLE)
1		M C H FT
2		M C H FT
3		M C H FT
4		M C H FT
5		M C H FT
6		M C H FT
7		M C H FT
8		M C H FT
9		M C H FT
10		M C H FT

PROSPECT GENERATION SHEET

M = Married   C = Children   H = Home Owner   FT = Full-Time Job

NAME	PHONE	NOTES (CIRCLE APPLICABLE)	
1			M C H FT
2			M C H FT
3			M C H FT
4			M C H FT
5			M C H FT
6			M C H FT
7			M C H FT
8			M C H FT
9			M C H FT
10			M C H FT

FOLLOW UP SHEET

NAME	PHONE	NOTES

WEEKLY ACTIVITY LOG / WEEK OF: _____

Be the Most Productive Person You Can Be At All Times

	SUNDAY	MONDAY	TUESDAY	WEDNESDAY	THURSDAY	FRIDAY	SATURDAY
8am							
9am							
10am							
11am							
12 noon							
1pm							
2pm							
3pm							
4pm							
5pm							
6pm							
7pm							
8pm							
9pm							

Persistence:

"Firm or obstinate continuance in a course of action in spite of difficulty or opposition."

Massive Action Plan To Get $_____ / Yr. Income
Weekly Activity Planner For The Week Of: _____

WEEKLY	GOAL	SUN	MON	TUE	WED	THU	FRI	SAT
PROSPECTS	20							
CALLS	100							
INTERVIEWS	15							
INVITES	10							
MEETINGS	10							
SIGN UPS								
SALES	$							
RESIDUALS	$							

MTD #'s	RECRUITS	RESIDUALS	SALES
PERSONAL			
TEAM			

PROSPECTS
1	
2	
3	
4	
5	
6	
7	
8	

MEETINGS
1	
2	
3	
4	
5	
6	
7	
8	
9	
10	

CALLS
1	
2	
3	
4	
5	
6	
7	
8	
9	
10	
11	
12	
13	
14	
15	

INTERVIEWS
1	
2	
3	
4	
5	
6	
7	
8	
9	
10	

DAILY MASSIVE ACTION PLAN

Goals & Affirmations For Day	Time:	Date:

DAILY SCHEDULE	PEOPLE TO CONTACT	THINGS TO DO
6:00am		
7:00am		
8:00am		
9:00am		
10:00am		
11:00am		
12:00 Noon		
1:00pm		
2:00pm		
3:00pm		
4:00pm		

DAILY SCHEDULE	ACTION TAKEN	GOAL	RESULT
5:00pm	PROSPECTS	3-10	
6:00pm	CALLS	20-30	
	INTERVIEWS	1-4	
9:00pm	INVITES	2-5	
	MEETINGS	2-3	
10:00pm	RESULTS CATEGORY	RESULTS	
	RECRUITS		
11:00pm	SALES		
	RESIDUALS		

PROSPECT GENERATION SHEET

M = Married   C = Children   H = Home Owner   FT = Full-Time Job

NAME	PHONE	NOTES (CIRCLE APPLICABLE)
1		M C H FT
2		M C H FT
3		M C H FT
4		M C H FT
5		M C H FT
6		M C H FT
7		M C H FT
8		M C H FT
9		M C H FT
10		M C H FT

PROSPECT GENERATION SHEET

M = Married   C = Children   H = Home Owner   FT = Full-Time Job

NAME	PHONE	NOTES (CIRCLE APPLICABLE)
1		M C H FT
2		M C H FT
3		M C H FT
4		M C H FT
5		M C H FT
6		M C H FT
7		M C H FT
8		M C H FT
9		M C H FT
10		M C H FT

FOLLOW UP SHEET

NAME	PHONE	NOTES

DAILY MASSIVE ACTION PLAN

Goals & Affirmations For Day	Time:	Date:

DAILY SCHEDULE	PEOPLE TO CONTACT	THINGS TO DO
6:00am		
7:00am		
8:00am		
9:00am		
10:00am		
11:00am		
12:00 Noon		
1:00pm		
2:00pm		
3:00pm		
4:00pm		

DAILY SCHEDULE	ACTION TAKEN	GOAL	RESULT
5:00pm	PROSPECTS	3-10	
6:00pm	CALLS	20-30	
	INTERVIEWS	1-4	
9:00pm	INVITES	2-5	
	MEETINGS	2-3	
10:00pm	RESULTS CATEGORY	RESULTS	
	RECRUITS		
11:00pm	SALES		
	RESIDUALS		

PROSPECT GENERATION SHEET

M = Married   C = Children   H = Home Owner   FT = Full-Time Job

NAME	PHONE	NOTES (CIRCLE APPLICABLE)
1		M C H FT
2		M C H FT
3		M C H FT
4		M C H FT
5		M C H FT
6		M C H FT
7		M C H FT
8		M C H FT
9		M C H FT
10		M C H FT

PROSPECT GENERATION SHEET

M = Married   C = Children   H = Home Owner   FT = Full-Time Job

NAME	PHONE	NOTES (CIRCLE APPLICABLE)
1		M C H FT
2		M C H FT
3		M C H FT
4		M C H FT
5		M C H FT
6		M C H FT
7		M C H FT
8		M C H FT
9		M C H FT
10		M C H FT

FOLLOW UP SHEET

NAME	PHONE	NOTES

DAILY MASSIVE ACTION PLAN

Goals & Affirmations For Day	Time:	Date:

DAILY SCHEDULE	PEOPLE TO CONTACT	THINGS TO DO
6:00am		
7:00am		
8:00am		
9:00am		
10:00am		
11:00am		
12:00 Noon		
1:00pm		
2:00pm		
3:00pm		
4:00pm		

DAILY SCHEDULE	ACTION TAKEN	GOAL	RESULT
5:00pm	PROSPECTS	3-10	
	CALLS	20-30	
6:00pm	INTERVIEWS	1-4	
	INVITES	2-5	
9:00pm	MEETINGS	2-3	

	RESULTS CATEGORY	RESULTS	
10:00pm	RECRUITS		
11:00pm	SALES		
	RESIDUALS		

PROSPECT GENERATION SHEET

M = Married   C = Children   H = Home Owner   FT = Full-Time Job

NAME	PHONE	NOTES (CIRCLE APPLICABLE)
1		M C H FT
2		M C H FT
3		M C H FT
4		M C H FT
5		M C H FT
6		M C H FT
7		M C H FT
8		M C H FT
9		M C H FT
10		M C H FT

PROSPECT GENERATION SHEET

M = Married   C = Children   H = Home Owner   FT = Full-Time Job

NAME	PHONE	NOTES (CIRCLE APPLICABLE)
1		M C H FT
2		M C H FT
3		M C H FT
4		M C H FT
5		M C H FT
6		M C H FT
7		M C H FT
8		M C H FT
9		M C H FT
10		M C H FT

FOLLOW UP SHEET

NAME	PHONE	NOTES

DAILY MASSIVE ACTION PLAN

Goals & Affirmations For Day	Time:	Date:

DAILY SCHEDULE	PEOPLE TO CONTACT	THINGS TO DO
6:00am		
7:00am		
8:00am		
9:00am		
10:00am		
11:00am		
12:00 Noon		
1:00pm		
2:00pm		
3:00pm		
4:00pm		

5:00pm	ACTION TAKEN	GOAL	RESULT
	PROSPECTS	3-10	
6:00pm	CALLS	20-30	
	INTERVIEWS	1-4	
9:00pm	INVITES	2-5	
	MEETINGS	2-3	
10:00pm	RESULTS CATEGORY	RESULTS	
	RECRUITS		
11:00pm	SALES		
	RESIDUALS		

PROSPECT GENERATION SHEET

M = Married   C = Children   H = Home Owner   FT = Full-Time Job

NAME	PHONE	NOTES (CIRCLE APPLICABLE)
1		M C H FT
2		M C H FT
3		M C H FT
4		M C H FT
5		M C H FT
6		M C H FT
7		M C H FT
8		M C H FT
9		M C H FT
10		M C H FT

PROSPECT GENERATION SHEET

M = Married   C = Children   H = Home Owner   FT = Full-Time Job

	NAME	PHONE	NOTES (CIRCLE APPLICABLE)
1			M C H FT
2			M C H FT
3			M C H FT
4			M C H FT
5			M C H FT
6			M C H FT
7			M C H FT
8			M C H FT
9			M C H FT
10			M C H FT

FOLLOW UP SHEET

NAME	PHONE	NOTES

DAILY MASSIVE ACTION PLAN

Goals & Affirmations For Day	Time:	Date:

DAILY SCHEDULE	PEOPLE TO CONTACT	THINGS TO DO
6:00am		
7:00am		
8:00am		
9:00am		
10:00am		
11:00am		
12:00 Noon		
1:00pm		
2:00pm		
3:00pm		
4:00pm		

DAILY SCHEDULE	ACTION TAKEN	GOAL	RESULT
5:00pm	PROSPECTS	3-10	
	CALLS	20-30	
6:00pm	INTERVIEWS	1-4	
	INVITES	2-5	
9:00pm	MEETINGS	2-3	

	RESULTS CATEGORY	RESULTS	
10:00pm	RECRUITS		
11:00pm	SALES		
	RESIDUALS		

PROSPECT GENERATION SHEET

M = Married   C = Children   H = Home Owner   FT = Full-Time Job

NAME	PHONE	NOTES (CIRCLE APPLICABLE)
1		M C H FT
2		M C H FT
3		M C H FT
4		M C H FT
5		M C H FT
6		M C H FT
7		M C H FT
8		M C H FT
9		M C H FT
10		M C H FT

PROSPECT GENERATION SHEET

M = Married   C = Children   H = Home Owner   FT = Full-Time Job

NAME	PHONE	NOTES (CIRCLE APPLICABLE)
1		M C H FT
2		M C H FT
3		M C H FT
4		M C H FT
5		M C H FT
6		M C H FT
7		M C H FT
8		M C H FT
9		M C H FT
10		M C H FT

FOLLOW UP SHEET

NAME	PHONE	NOTES

DAILY MASSIVE ACTION PLAN

Goals & Affirmations For Day	Time:		Date:	

DAILY SCHEDULE	PEOPLE TO CONTACT	THINGS TO DO
6:00am		
7:00am		
8:00am		
9:00am		
10:00am		
11:00am		
12:00 Noon		
1:00pm		
2:00pm		
3:00pm		
4:00pm		

	ACTION TAKEN	GOAL	RESULT
5:00pm	PROSPECTS	3-10	
6:00pm	CALLS	20-30	
	INTERVIEWS	1-4	
9:00pm	INVITES	2-5	
	MEETINGS	2-3	
10:00pm	RESULTS CATEGORY	RESULTS	
	RECRUITS		
11:00pm	SALES		
	RESIDUALS		

PROSPECT GENERATION SHEET

M = Married   C = Children   H = Home Owner   FT = Full-Time Job

NAME	PHONE	NOTES (CIRCLE APPLICABLE)
1		M C H FT
2		M C H FT
3		M C H FT
4		M C H FT
5		M C H FT
6		M C H FT
7		M C H FT
8		M C H FT
9		M C H FT
10		M C H FT

PROSPECT GENERATION SHEET

M = Married   C = Children   H = Home Owner   FT = Full-Time Job

NAME	PHONE	NOTES (CIRCLE APPLICABLE)	
1			M C H FT
2			M C H FT
3			M C H FT
4			M C H FT
5			M C H FT
6			M C H FT
7			M C H FT
8			M C H FT
9			M C H FT
10			M C H FT

FOLLOW UP SHEET

NAME	PHONE	NOTES

DAILY MASSIVE ACTION PLAN

Goals & Affirmations For Day	Time:	Date:

DAILY SCHEDULE	PEOPLE TO CONTACT	THINGS TO DO
6:00am		
7:00am		
8:00am		
9:00am		
10:00am		
11:00am		
12:00 Noon		
1:00pm		
2:00pm		
3:00pm		
4:00pm		

DAILY SCHEDULE	ACTION TAKEN	GOAL	RESULT
5:00pm	PROSPECTS	3-10	
6:00pm	CALLS	20-30	
	INTERVIEWS	1-4	
9:00pm	INVITES	2-5	
	MEETINGS	2-3	

DAILY SCHEDULE	RESULTS CATEGORY	RESULTS
10:00pm	RECRUITS	
11:00pm	SALES	
	RESIDUALS	

PROSPECT GENERATION SHEET

M = Married   C = Children   H = Home Owner   FT = Full-Time Job

NAME	PHONE	NOTES (CIRCLE APPLICABLE)
1		M C H FT
2		M C H FT
3		M C H FT
4		M C H FT
5		M C H FT
6		M C H FT
7		M C H FT
8		M C H FT
9		M C H FT
10		M C H FT

PROSPECT GENERATION SHEET

M = Married   C = Children   H = Home Owner   FT = Full-Time Job

NAME	PHONE	NOTES (CIRCLE APPLICABLE)
1		M C H FT
2		M C H FT
3		M C H FT
4		M C H FT
5		M C H FT
6		M C H FT
7		M C H FT
8		M C H FT
9		M C H FT
10		M C H FT

FOLLOW UP SHEET

NAME	PHONE	NOTES

WEEKLY ACTIVITY LOG / WEEK OF: _____

Be the Most Productive Person You Can Be At All Times

	SUNDAY	MONDAY	TUESDAY	WEDNESDAY	THURSDAY	FRIDAY	SATURDAY
8am							
9am							
10am							
11am							
12 noon							
1pm							
2pm							
3pm							
4pm							
5pm							
6pm							
7pm							
8pm							
9pm							

Persistence:

"Firm or obstinate continuance in a course of action in spite of difficulty or opposition."

Massive Action Plan To Get $_____ / Yr. Income
Weekly Activity Planner For The Week Of: _____

WEEKLY	GOAL	SUN	MON	TUE	WED	THU	FRI	SAT
PROSPECTS	20							
CALLS	100							
INTERVIEWS	15							
INVITES	10							
MEETINGS	10							
SIGN UPS								
SALES	$							
RESIDUALS	$							

MTD #'s	RECRUITS	RESIDUALS	SALES
PERSONAL			
TEAM			

PROSPECTS
1
2
3
4
5
6
7
8

MEETINGS
1
2
3
4
5
6
7
8
9
10

CALLS
1
2
3
4
5
6
7
8
9
10
11
12
13
14
15

INTERVIEWS
1
2
3
4
5
6
7
8
9
10

DAILY MASSIVE ACTION PLAN

Goals & Affirmations For Day	Time:	Date:

DAILY SCHEDULE	PEOPLE TO CONTACT	THINGS TO DO
6:00am		
7:00am		
8:00am		
9:00am		
10:00am		
11:00am		
12:00 Noon		
1:00pm		
2:00pm		
3:00pm		
4:00pm		

DAILY SCHEDULE	ACTION TAKEN	GOAL	RESULT
5:00pm	PROSPECTS	3-10	
6:00pm	CALLS	20-30	
	INTERVIEWS	1-4	
9:00pm	INVITES	2-5	
	MEETINGS	2-3	
10:00pm	RESULTS CATEGORY	RESULTS	
	RECRUITS		
11:00pm	SALES		
	RESIDUALS		

PROSPECT GENERATION SHEET

M = Married   C = Children   H = Home Owner   FT = Full-Time Job

NAME	PHONE	NOTES (CIRCLE APPLICABLE)	
1			M C H FT
2			M C H FT
3			M C H FT
4			M C H FT
5			M C H FT
6			M C H FT
7			M C H FT
8			M C H FT
9			M C H FT
10			M C H FT

PROSPECT GENERATION SHEET

M = Married   C = Children   H = Home Owner   FT = Full-Time Job

NAME	PHONE	NOTES (CIRCLE APPLICABLE)	
1			M C H FT
2			M C H FT
3			M C H FT
4			M C H FT
5			M C H FT
6			M C H FT
7			M C H FT
8			M C H FT
9			M C H FT
10			M C H FT

FOLLOW UP SHEET

NAME	PHONE	NOTES

DAILY MASSIVE ACTION PLAN

Goals & Affirmations For Day		Time:		Date:	

DAILY SCHEDULE	PEOPLE TO CONTACT	THINGS TO DO
6:00am		
7:00am		
8:00am		
9:00am		
10:00am		
11:00am		
12:00 Noon		
1:00pm		
2:00pm		
3:00pm		
4:00pm		

5:00pm	ACTION TAKEN	GOAL	RESULT
	PROSPECTS	3-10	
6:00pm	CALLS	20-30	
	INTERVIEWS	1-4	
9:00pm	INVITES	2-5	
	MEETINGS	2-3	

10:00pm	RESULTS CATEGORY	RESULTS
	RECRUITS	
11:00pm	SALES	
	RESIDUALS	

PROSPECT GENERATION SHEET

M = Married   C = Children   H = Home Owner   FT = Full-Time Job

NAME	PHONE	NOTES (CIRCLE APPLICABLE)	
1			M C H FT
2			M C H FT
3			M C H FT
4			M C H FT
5			M C H FT
6			M C H FT
7			M C H FT
8			M C H FT
9			M C H FT
10			M C H FT

PROSPECT GENERATION SHEET

M = Married   C = Children   H = Home Owner   FT = Full-Time Job

NAME	PHONE	NOTES (CIRCLE APPLICABLE)
1		M C H FT
2		M C H FT
3		M C H FT
4		M C H FT
5		M C H FT
6		M C H FT
7		M C H FT
8		M C H FT
9		M C H FT
10		M C H FT

FOLLOW UP SHEET

NAME	PHONE	NOTES

DAILY MASSIVE ACTION PLAN

Goals & Affirmations For Day	Time:		Date:	

DAILY SCHEDULE	PEOPLE TO CONTACT	THINGS TO DO
6:00am		
7:00am		
8:00am		
9:00am		
10:00am		
11:00am		
12:00 Noon		
1:00pm		
2:00pm		
3:00pm		
4:00pm		

	ACTION TAKEN	GOAL	RESULT
5:00pm	PROSPECTS	3-10	
6:00pm	CALLS	20-30	
	INTERVIEWS	1-4	
9:00pm	INVITES	2-5	
	MEETINGS	2-3	

	RESULTS CATEGORY	RESULTS
10:00pm	RECRUITS	
11:00pm	SALES	
	RESIDUALS	

PROSPECT GENERATION SHEET

M = Married   C = Children   H = Home Owner   FT = Full-Time Job

NAME	PHONE	NOTES (CIRCLE APPLICABLE)	
1			M C H FT
2			M C H FT
3			M C H FT
4			M C H FT
5			M C H FT
6			M C H FT
7			M C H FT
8			M C H FT
9			M C H FT
10			M C H FT

PROSPECT GENERATION SHEET

M = Married   C = Children   H = Home Owner   FT = Full-Time Job

NAME	PHONE	NOTES (CIRCLE APPLICABLE)
1		M C H FT
2		M C H FT
3		M C H FT
4		M C H FT
5		M C H FT
6		M C H FT
7		M C H FT
8		M C H FT
9		M C H FT
10		M C H FT

FOLLOW UP SHEET

NAME	PHONE	NOTES

DAILY MASSIVE ACTION PLAN

Goals & Affirmations For Day	Time:	Date:

DAILY SCHEDULE	PEOPLE TO CONTACT	THINGS TO DO
6:00am		
7:00am		
8:00am		
9:00am		
10:00am		
11:00am		
12:00 Noon		
1:00pm		
2:00pm		
3:00pm		
4:00pm		

DAILY SCHEDULE	ACTION TAKEN	GOAL	RESULT
5:00pm	PROSPECTS	3-10	
6:00pm	CALLS	20-30	
	INTERVIEWS	1-4	
9:00pm	INVITES	2-5	
	MEETINGS	2-3	
10:00pm	RESULTS CATEGORY	RESULTS	
	RECRUITS		
11:00pm	SALES		
	RESIDUALS		

PROSPECT GENERATION SHEET

M = Married   C = Children   H = Home Owner   FT = Full-Time Job

NAME	PHONE	NOTES (CIRCLE APPLICABLE)	
1			M C H FT
2			M C H FT
3			M C H FT
4			M C H FT
5			M C H FT
6			M C H FT
7			M C H FT
8			M C H FT
9			M C H FT
10			M C H FT

PROSPECT GENERATION SHEET

M = Married   C = Children   H = Home Owner   FT = Full-Time Job

NAME	PHONE	NOTES (CIRCLE APPLICABLE)
1		M C H FT
2		M C H FT
3		M C H FT
4		M C H FT
5		M C H FT
6		M C H FT
7		M C H FT
8		M C H FT
9		M C H FT
10		M C H FT

FOLLOW UP SHEET

NAME	PHONE	NOTES

DAILY MASSIVE ACTION PLAN

Goals & Affirmations For Day	Time:	Date:

DAILY SCHEDULE	PEOPLE TO CONTACT	THINGS TO DO
6:00am		
7:00am		
8:00am		
9:00am		
10:00am		
11:00am		
12:00 Noon		
1:00pm		
2:00pm		
3:00pm		
4:00pm		

	ACTION TAKEN	GOAL	RESULT
5:00pm	PROSPECTS	3-10	
6:00pm	CALLS	20-30	
	INTERVIEWS	1-4	
9:00pm	INVITES	2-5	
	MEETINGS	2-3	

	RESULTS CATEGORY	RESULTS	
10:00pm	RECRUITS		
11:00pm	SALES		
	RESIDUALS		

PROSPECT GENERATION SHEET

M = Married   C = Children   H = Home Owner   FT = Full-Time Job

NAME	PHONE	NOTES (CIRCLE APPLICABLE)
1		M C H FT
2		M C H FT
3		M C H FT
4		M C H FT
5		M C H FT
6		M C H FT
7		M C H FT
8		M C H FT
9		M C H FT
10		M C H FT

PROSPECT GENERATION SHEET

M = Married   C = Children   H = Home Owner   FT = Full-Time Job

NAME	PHONE	NOTES (CIRCLE APPLICABLE)
1		M C H FT
2		M C H FT
3		M C H FT
4		M C H FT
5		M C H FT
6		M C H FT
7		M C H FT
8		M C H FT
9		M C H FT
10		M C H FT

FOLLOW UP SHEET

NAME	PHONE	NOTES

DAILY MASSIVE ACTION PLAN

Goals & Affirmations For Day	Time:	Date:

DAILY SCHEDULE	PEOPLE TO CONTACT	THINGS TO DO
6:00am		
7:00am		
8:00am		
9:00am		
10:00am		
11:00am		
12:00 Noon		
1:00pm		
2:00pm		
3:00pm		
4:00pm		

DAILY SCHEDULE	ACTION TAKEN	GOAL	RESULT
5:00pm	PROSPECTS	3-10	
6:00pm	CALLS	20-30	
	INTERVIEWS	1-4	
9:00pm	INVITES	2-5	
	MEETINGS	2-3	
10:00pm	RESULTS CATEGORY	RESULTS	
	RECRUITS		
11:00pm	SALES		
	RESIDUALS		

PROSPECT GENERATION SHEET

M = Married   C = Children   H = Home Owner   FT = Full-Time Job

NAME	PHONE	NOTES (CIRCLE APPLICABLE)	
1			M C H FT
2			M C H FT
3			M C H FT
4			M C H FT
5			M C H FT
6			M C H FT
7			M C H FT
8			M C H FT
9			M C H FT
10			M C H FT

PROSPECT GENERATION SHEET

M = Married   C = Children   H = Home Owner   FT = Full-Time Job

NAME	PHONE	NOTES (CIRCLE APPLICABLE)
1		M C H FT
2		M C H FT
3		M C H FT
4		M C H FT
5		M C H FT
6		M C H FT
7		M C H FT
8		M C H FT
9		M C H FT
10		M C H FT

FOLLOW UP SHEET

NAME	PHONE	NOTES

DAILY MASSIVE ACTION PLAN

Goals & Affirmations For Day	Time:	Date:

DAILY SCHEDULE	PEOPLE TO CONTACT	THINGS TO DO
6:00am		
7:00am		
8:00am		
9:00am		
10:00am		
11:00am		
12:00 Noon		
1:00pm		
2:00pm		
3:00pm		
4:00pm		

	ACTION TAKEN	GOAL	RESULT
5:00pm	PROSPECTS	3-10	
6:00pm	CALLS	20-30	
	INTERVIEWS	1-4	
9:00pm	INVITES	2-5	
	MEETINGS	2-3	

	RESULTS CATEGORY	RESULTS
10:00pm	RECRUITS	
11:00pm	SALES	
	RESIDUALS	

PROSPECT GENERATION SHEET

M = Married   C = Children   H = Home Owner   FT = Full-Time Job

NAME	PHONE	NOTES (CIRCLE APPLICABLE)
1		M C H FT
2		M C H FT
3		M C H FT
4		M C H FT
5		M C H FT
6		M C H FT
7		M C H FT
8		M C H FT
9		M C H FT
10		M C H FT

PROSPECT GENERATION SHEET

M = Married   C = Children   H = Home Owner   FT = Full-Time Job

NAME	PHONE	NOTES (CIRCLE APPLICABLE)
1		M C H FT
2		M C H FT
3		M C H FT
4		M C H FT
5		M C H FT
6		M C H FT
7		M C H FT
8		M C H FT
9		M C H FT
10		M C H FT

FOLLOW UP SHEET

NAME	PHONE	NOTES

WEEKLY ACTIVITY LOG / WEEK OF: _____

Be the Most Productive Person You Can Be At All Times

	SUNDAY	MONDAY	TUESDAY	WEDNESDAY	THURSDAY	FRIDAY	SATURDAY
8am							
9am							
10am							
11am							
12 noon							
1pm							
2pm							
3pm							
4pm							
5pm							
6pm							
7pm							
8pm							
9pm							

Persistence:

"Firm or obstinate continuance in a course of action in spite of difficulty or opposition."

Massive Action Plan To Get $_____ / Yr. Income

Weekly Activity Planner For The Week Of: _____

WEEKLY	GOAL	SUN	MON	TUE	WED	THU	FRI	SAT
PROSPECTS	20							
CALLS	100							
INTERVIEWS	15							
INVITES	10							
MEETINGS	10							
SIGN UPS								
SALES	$							
RESIDUALS	$							

MTD #'s	RECRUITS	RESIDUALS	SALES
PERSONAL			
TEAM			

PROSPECTS
1
2
3
4
5
6
7
8

MEETINGS
1
2
3
4
5
6
7
8
9
10

CALLS
1
2
3
4
5
6
7
8
9
10
11
12
13
14
15

INTERVIEWS
1
2
3
4
5
6
7
8
9
10

DAILY MASSIVE ACTION PLAN

Goals & Affirmations For Day	Time:	Date:

DAILY SCHEDULE	PEOPLE TO CONTACT	THINGS TO DO
6:00am		
7:00am		
8:00am		
9:00am		
10:00am		
11:00am		
12:00 Noon		
1:00pm		
2:00pm		
3:00pm		
4:00pm		

DAILY SCHEDULE	ACTION TAKEN	GOAL	RESULT
5:00pm	PROSPECTS	3-10	
	CALLS	20-30	
6:00pm	INTERVIEWS	1-4	
	INVITES	2-5	
9:00pm	MEETINGS	2-3	

	RESULTS CATEGORY	RESULTS
10:00pm	RECRUITS	
	SALES	
11:00pm	RESIDUALS	

PROSPECT GENERATION SHEET

M = Married   C = Children   H = Home Owner   FT = Full-Time Job

NAME	PHONE	NOTES (CIRCLE APPLICABLE)
1		M C H FT
2		M C H FT
3		M C H FT
4		M C H FT
5		M C H FT
6		M C H FT
7		M C H FT
8		M C H FT
9		M C H FT
10		M C H FT

PROSPECT GENERATION SHEET

M = Married   C = Children   H = Home Owner   FT = Full-Time Job

NAME	PHONE	NOTES (CIRCLE APPLICABLE)
1		M C H FT
2		M C H FT
3		M C H FT
4		M C H FT
5		M C H FT
6		M C H FT
7		M C H FT
8		M C H FT
9		M C H FT
10		M C H FT

FOLLOW UP SHEET

NAME	PHONE	NOTES

DAILY MASSIVE ACTION PLAN

Goals & Affirmations For Day	Time:	Date:

DAILY SCHEDULE	PEOPLE TO CONTACT	THINGS TO DO
6:00am		
7:00am		
8:00am		
9:00am		
10:00am		
11:00am		
12:00 Noon		
1:00pm		
2:00pm		
3:00pm		
4:00pm		

	ACTION TAKEN	GOAL	RESULT
5:00pm	PROSPECTS	3-10	
6:00pm	CALLS	20-30	
	INTERVIEWS	1-4	
9:00pm	INVITES	2-5	
	MEETINGS	2-3	

	RESULTS CATEGORY	RESULTS
10:00pm	RECRUITS	
11:00pm	SALES	
	RESIDUALS	

PROSPECT GENERATION SHEET

M = Married   C = Children   H = Home Owner   FT = Full-Time Job

NAME	PHONE	NOTES (CIRCLE APPLICABLE)
1		M C H FT
2		M C H FT
3		M C H FT
4		M C H FT
5		M C H FT
6		M C H FT
7		M C H FT
8		M C H FT
9		M C H FT
10		M C H FT

PROSPECT GENERATION SHEET

M = Married   C = Children   H = Home Owner   FT = Full-Time Job

NAME	PHONE	NOTES (CIRCLE APPLICABLE)
1		M C H FT
2		M C H FT
3		M C H FT
4		M C H FT
5		M C H FT
6		M C H FT
7		M C H FT
8		M C H FT
9		M C H FT
10		M C H FT

FOLLOW UP SHEET

NAME	PHONE	NOTES

DAILY MASSIVE ACTION PLAN

Goals & Affirmations For Day	Time:	Date:

DAILY SCHEDULE	PEOPLE TO CONTACT	THINGS TO DO
6:00am		
7:00am		
8:00am		
9:00am		
10:00am		
11:00am		
12:00 Noon		
1:00pm		
2:00pm		
3:00pm		
4:00pm		

DAILY SCHEDULE	ACTION TAKEN	GOAL	RESULT
5:00pm	PROSPECTS	3-10	
6:00pm	CALLS	20-30	
	INTERVIEWS	1-4	
9:00pm	INVITES	2-5	
	MEETINGS	2-3	

	RESULTS CATEGORY	RESULTS	
10:00pm	RECRUITS		
	SALES		
11:00pm	RESIDUALS		

PROSPECT GENERATION SHEET

M = Married   C = Children   H = Home Owner   FT = Full-Time Job

NAME	PHONE	NOTES (CIRCLE APPLICABLE)	
1			M C H FT
2			M C H FT
3			M C H FT
4			M C H FT
5			M C H FT
6			M C H FT
7			M C H FT
8			M C H FT
9			M C H FT
10			M C H FT

PROSPECT GENERATION SHEET

M = Married   C = Children   H = Home Owner   FT = Full-Time Job

NAME	PHONE	NOTES (CIRCLE APPLICABLE)
1		M C H FT
2		M C H FT
3		M C H FT
4		M C H FT
5		M C H FT
6		M C H FT
7		M C H FT
8		M C H FT
9		M C H FT
10		M C H FT

FOLLOW UP SHEET

NAME	PHONE	NOTES

DAILY MASSIVE ACTION PLAN

Goals & Affirmations For Day	Time:	Date:

DAILY SCHEDULE	PEOPLE TO CONTACT	THINGS TO DO
6:00am		
7:00am		
8:00am		
9:00am		
10:00am		
11:00am		
12:00 Noon		
1:00pm		
2:00pm		
3:00pm		
4:00pm		

DAILY SCHEDULE	ACTION TAKEN	GOAL	RESULT
5:00pm	PROSPECTS	3-10	
6:00pm	CALLS	20-30	
	INTERVIEWS	1-4	
9:00pm	INVITES	2-5	
	MEETINGS	2-3	

	RESULTS CATEGORY	RESULTS	
10:00pm	RECRUITS		
11:00pm	SALES		
	RESIDUALS		

PROSPECT GENERATION SHEET

M = Married   C = Children   H = Home Owner   FT = Full-Time Job

NAME	PHONE	NOTES (CIRCLE APPLICABLE)
1		M C H FT
2		M C H FT
3		M C H FT
4		M C H FT
5		M C H FT
6		M C H FT
7		M C H FT
8		M C H FT
9		M C H FT
10		M C H FT

PROSPECT GENERATION SHEET

M = Married   C = Children   H = Home Owner   FT = Full-Time Job

NAME	PHONE	NOTES (CIRCLE APPLICABLE)
1		M C H FT
2		M C H FT
3		M C H FT
4		M C H FT
5		M C H FT
6		M C H FT
7		M C H FT
8		M C H FT
9		M C H FT
10		M C H FT

FOLLOW UP SHEET

NAME	PHONE	NOTES

DAILY MASSIVE ACTION PLAN

Goals & Affirmations For Day	Time:	Date:

DAILY SCHEDULE	PEOPLE TO CONTACT	THINGS TO DO
6:00am		
7:00am		
8:00am		
9:00am		
10:00am		
11:00am		
12:00 Noon		
1:00pm		
2:00pm		
3:00pm		
4:00pm		

DAILY SCHEDULE	ACTION TAKEN	GOAL	RESULT
5:00pm	PROSPECTS	3-10	
6:00pm	CALLS	20-30	
	INTERVIEWS	1-4	
9:00pm	INVITES	2-5	
	MEETINGS	2-3	
10:00pm	RESULTS CATEGORY	RESULTS	
	RECRUITS		
11:00pm	SALES		
	RESIDUALS		

PROSPECT GENERATION SHEET

M = Married   C = Children   H = Home Owner   FT = Full-Time Job

NAME	PHONE	NOTES (CIRCLE APPLICABLE)	
1			M C H FT
2			M C H FT
3			M C H FT
4			M C H FT
5			M C H FT
6			M C H FT
7			M C H FT
8			M C H FT
9			M C H FT
10			M C H FT

PROSPECT GENERATION SHEET

M = Married   C = Children   H = Home Owner   FT = Full-Time Job

NAME	PHONE	NOTES (CIRCLE APPLICABLE)	
1			M C H FT
2			M C H FT
3			M C H FT
4			M C H FT
5			M C H FT
6			M C H FT
7			M C H FT
8			M C H FT
9			M C H FT
10			M C H FT

FOLLOW UP SHEET

NAME	PHONE	NOTES

DAILY MASSIVE ACTION PLAN

Goals & Affirmations For Day	Time:	Date:

DAILY SCHEDULE	PEOPLE TO CONTACT	THINGS TO DO
6:00am		
7:00am		
8:00am		
9:00am		
10:00am		
11:00am		
12:00 Noon		
1:00pm		
2:00pm		
3:00pm		
4:00pm		

DAILY SCHEDULE	ACTION TAKEN	GOAL	RESULT
5:00pm	PROSPECTS	3-10	
6:00pm	CALLS	20-30	
	INTERVIEWS	1-4	
9:00pm	INVITES	2-5	
	MEETINGS	2-3	
10:00pm	RESULTS CATEGORY	RESULTS	
	RECRUITS		
11:00pm	SALES		
	RESIDUALS		

PROSPECT GENERATION SHEET

M = Married   C = Children   H = Home Owner   FT = Full-Time Job

NAME	PHONE	NOTES (CIRCLE APPLICABLE)
1		M C H FT
2		M C H FT
3		M C H FT
4		M C H FT
5		M C H FT
6		M C H FT
7		M C H FT
8		M C H FT
9		M C H FT
10		M C H FT

PROSPECT GENERATION SHEET

M = Married   C = Children   H = Home Owner   FT = Full-Time Job

NAME	PHONE	NOTES (CIRCLE APPLICABLE)	
1			M C H FT
2			M C H FT
3			M C H FT
4			M C H FT
5			M C H FT
6			M C H FT
7			M C H FT
8			M C H FT
9			M C H FT
10			M C H FT

FOLLOW UP SHEET

NAME	PHONE	NOTES

DAILY MASSIVE ACTION PLAN

Goals & Affirmations For Day	Time:	Date:

DAILY SCHEDULE	PEOPLE TO CONTACT	THINGS TO DO
6:00am		
7:00am		
8:00am		
9:00am		
10:00am		
11:00am		
12:00 Noon		
1:00pm		
2:00pm		
3:00pm		
4:00pm		

DAILY SCHEDULE	ACTION TAKEN	GOAL	RESULT
5:00pm	PROSPECTS	3-10	
6:00pm	CALLS	20-30	
	INTERVIEWS	1-4	
9:00pm	INVITES	2-5	
	MEETINGS	2-3	
10:00pm	RESULTS CATEGORY	RESULTS	
	RECRUITS		
11:00pm	SALES		
	RESIDUALS		

PROSPECT GENERATION SHEET

M = Married   C = Children   H = Home Owner   FT = Full-Time Job

NAME	PHONE	NOTES (CIRCLE APPLICABLE)	
1			M C H FT
2			M C H FT
3			M C H FT
4			M C H FT
5			M C H FT
6			M C H FT
7			M C H FT
8			M C H FT
9			M C H FT
10			M C H FT

PROSPECT GENERATION SHEET

M = Married   C = Children   H = Home Owner   FT = Full-Time Job

NAME	PHONE	NOTES (CIRCLE APPLICABLE)
1		M C H FT
2		M C H FT
3		M C H FT
4		M C H FT
5		M C H FT
6		M C H FT
7		M C H FT
8		M C H FT
9		M C H FT
10		M C H FT

FOLLOW UP SHEET

NAME	PHONE	NOTES

MONTH OF: _____

SUNDAY	MONDAY	TUESDAY	WEDNESDAY	THURSDAY	FRIDAY	SATURDAY

Monthly Goals	
Personal Sales	
Team Sales	
Personal Recruits	
Team Recruits	
Monthly Sales Income	
Monthly Residual Income	

Monthly Results	
Personal Sales	
Team Sales	
Personal Recruits	
Team Recruits	
Monthly Sales Income	
Monthly Residual Income	

Month End Review

_____

_____

_____

_____

90-Day Run Notes

WEEKLY ACTIVITY LOG / WEEK OF: _____

Be the Most Productive Person You Can Be At All Times

	SUNDAY	MONDAY	TUESDAY	WEDNESDAY	THURSDAY	FRIDAY	SATURDAY
8am							
9am							
10am							
11am							
12 noon							
1pm							
2pm							
3pm							
4pm							
5pm							
6pm							
7pm							
8pm							
9pm							

Persistence:

"Firm or obstinate continuance in a course of action in spite of difficulty or opposition."

Massive Action Plan To Get $_____ / Yr. Income
Weekly Activity Planner For The Week Of: _____

WEEKLY	GOAL	SUN	MON	TUE	WED	THU	FRI	SAT
PROSPECTS	20							
CALLS	100							
INTERVIEWS	15							
INVITES	10							
MEETINGS	10							
SIGN UPS								
SALES	$							
RESIDUALS	$							

MTD #'s	RECRUITS	RESIDUALS	SALES
PERSONAL			
TEAM			

PROSPECTS
1
2
3
4
5
6
7
8

MEETINGS
1
2
3
4
5
6
7
8
9
10

INTERVIEWS
1
2
3
4
5
6
7
8
9
10

CALLS
1
2
3
4
5
6
7
8
9
10
11
12
13
14
15

DAILY MASSIVE ACTION PLAN

Goals & Affirmations For Day	Time:	Date:

DAILY SCHEDULE	PEOPLE TO CONTACT	THINGS TO DO
6:00am		
7:00am		
8:00am		
9:00am		
10:00am		
11:00am		
12:00 Noon		
1:00pm		
2:00pm		
3:00pm		
4:00pm		

DAILY SCHEDULE	ACTION TAKEN	GOAL	RESULT
5:00pm	PROSPECTS	3-10	
	CALLS	20-30	
6:00pm	INTERVIEWS	1-4	
	INVITES	2-5	
9:00pm	MEETINGS	2-3	
10:00pm	RESULTS CATEGORY	RESULTS	
	RECRUITS		
11:00pm	SALES		
	RESIDUALS		

PROSPECT GENERATION SHEET

M = Married   C = Children   H = Home Owner   FT = Full-Time Job

NAME	PHONE	NOTES (CIRCLE APPLICABLE)	
1			M C H FT
2			M C H FT
3			M C H FT
4			M C H FT
5			M C H FT
6			M C H FT
7			M C H FT
8			M C H FT
9			M C H FT
10			M C H FT

PROSPECT GENERATION SHEET

M = Married   C = Children   H = Home Owner   FT = Full-Time Job

NAME	PHONE	NOTES (CIRCLE APPLICABLE)	
1			M C H FT
2			M C H FT
3			M C H FT
4			M C H FT
5			M C H FT
6			M C H FT
7			M C H FT
8			M C H FT
9			M C H FT
10			M C H FT

FOLLOW UP SHEET

NAME	PHONE	NOTES

DAILY MASSIVE ACTION PLAN

Goals & Affirmations For Day	Time:	Date:

DAILY SCHEDULE	PEOPLE TO CONTACT	THINGS TO DO
6:00am		
7:00am		
8:00am		
9:00am		
10:00am		
11:00am		
12:00 Noon		
1:00pm		
2:00pm		
3:00pm		
4:00pm		

DAILY SCHEDULE	ACTION TAKEN	GOAL	RESULT
5:00pm	PROSPECTS	3-10	
	CALLS	20-30	
6:00pm	INTERVIEWS	1-4	
	INVITES	2-5	
9:00pm	MEETINGS	2-3	
10:00pm	RESULTS CATEGORY	RESULTS	
	RECRUITS		
11:00pm	SALES		
	RESIDUALS		

PROSPECT GENERATION SHEET

M = Married   C = Children   H = Home Owner   FT = Full-Time Job

NAME	PHONE	NOTES (CIRCLE APPLICABLE)
1		M C H FT
2		M C H FT
3		M C H FT
4		M C H FT
5		M C H FT
6		M C H FT
7		M C H FT
8		M C H FT
9		M C H FT
10		M C H FT

PROSPECT GENERATION SHEET

M = Married   C = Children   H = Home Owner   FT = Full-Time Job

NAME	PHONE	NOTES (CIRCLE APPLICABLE)
1		M C H FT
2		M C H FT
3		M C H FT
4		M C H FT
5		M C H FT
6		M C H FT
7		M C H FT
8		M C H FT
9		M C H FT
10		M C H FT

FOLLOW UP SHEET

NAME	PHONE	NOTES

DAILY MASSIVE ACTION PLAN

Goals & Affirmations For Day	Time:	Date:

DAILY SCHEDULE	PEOPLE TO CONTACT	THINGS TO DO
6:00am		
7:00am		
8:00am		
9:00am		
10:00am		
11:00am		
12:00 Noon		
1:00pm		
2:00pm		
3:00pm		
4:00pm		

	ACTION TAKEN	GOAL	RESULT
5:00pm	PROSPECTS	3-10	
6:00pm	CALLS	20-30	
	INTERVIEWS	1-4	
9:00pm	INVITES	2-5	
	MEETINGS	2-3	

	RESULTS CATEGORY	RESULTS
10:00pm	RECRUITS	
	SALES	
11:00pm	RESIDUALS	

PROSPECT GENERATION SHEET

M = Married   C = Children   H = Home Owner   FT = Full-Time Job

NAME	PHONE	NOTES (CIRCLE APPLICABLE)	
1			M C H FT
2			M C H FT
3			M C H FT
4			M C H FT
5			M C H FT
6			M C H FT
7			M C H FT
8			M C H FT
9			M C H FT
10			M C H FT

PROSPECT GENERATION SHEET

M = Married   C = Children   H = Home Owner   FT = Full-Time Job

NAME	PHONE	NOTES (CIRCLE APPLICABLE)
1		M C H FT
2		M C H FT
3		M C H FT
4		M C H FT
5		M C H FT
6		M C H FT
7		M C H FT
8		M C H FT
9		M C H FT
10		M C H FT

FOLLOW UP SHEET

NAME	PHONE	NOTES

DAILY MASSIVE ACTION PLAN

Goals & Affirmations For Day	Time:	Date:

DAILY SCHEDULE	PEOPLE TO CONTACT	THINGS TO DO
6:00am		
7:00am		
8:00am		
9:00am		
10:00am		
11:00am		
12:00 Noon		
1:00pm		
2:00pm		
3:00pm		
4:00pm		

DAILY SCHEDULE	ACTION TAKEN	GOAL	RESULT
5:00pm	PROSPECTS	3-10	
6:00pm	CALLS	20-30	
	INTERVIEWS	1-4	
9:00pm	INVITES	2-5	
	MEETINGS	2-3	

	RESULTS CATEGORY	RESULTS	
10:00pm	RECRUITS		
11:00pm	SALES		
	RESIDUALS		

PROSPECT GENERATION SHEET

M = Married   C = Children   H = Home Owner   FT = Full-Time Job

NAME	PHONE	NOTES (CIRCLE APPLICABLE)
1		M C H FT
2		M C H FT
3		M C H FT
4		M C H FT
5		M C H FT
6		M C H FT
7		M C H FT
8		M C H FT
9		M C H FT
10		M C H FT

PROSPECT GENERATION SHEET

M = Married   C = Children   H = Home Owner   FT = Full-Time Job

NAME	PHONE	NOTES (CIRCLE APPLICABLE)
1		M C H FT
2		M C H FT
3		M C H FT
4		M C H FT
5		M C H FT
6		M C H FT
7		M C H FT
8		M C H FT
9		M C H FT
10		M C H FT

FOLLOW UP SHEET

NAME	PHONE	NOTES

DAILY MASSIVE ACTION PLAN

Goals & Affirmations For Day		Time:		Date:	

DAILY SCHEDULE	PEOPLE TO CONTACT	THINGS TO DO
6:00am		
7:00am		
8:00am		
9:00am		
10:00am		
11:00am		
12:00 Noon		
1:00pm		
2:00pm		
3:00pm		
4:00pm		

DAILY SCHEDULE	ACTION TAKEN	GOAL	RESULT
5:00pm	PROSPECTS	3-10	
6:00pm	CALLS	20-30	
	INTERVIEWS	1-4	
9:00pm	INVITES	2-5	
	MEETINGS	2-3	
10:00pm	RESULTS CATEGORY	RESULTS	
	RECRUITS		
11:00pm	SALES		
	RESIDUALS		

PROSPECT GENERATION SHEET

M = Married   C = Children   H = Home Owner   FT = Full-Time Job

NAME	PHONE	NOTES (CIRCLE APPLICABLE)
1		M C H FT
2		M C H FT
3		M C H FT
4		M C H FT
5		M C H FT
6		M C H FT
7		M C H FT
8		M C H FT
9		M C H FT
10		M C H FT

PROSPECT GENERATION SHEET

M = Married   C = Children   H = Home Owner   FT = Full-Time Job

NAME	PHONE	NOTES (CIRCLE APPLICABLE)
1		M C H FT
2		M C H FT
3		M C H FT
4		M C H FT
5		M C H FT
6		M C H FT
7		M C H FT
8		M C H FT
9		M C H FT
10		M C H FT

FOLLOW UP SHEET

NAME	PHONE	NOTES

DAILY MASSIVE ACTION PLAN

Goals & Affirmations For Day	Time:	Date:

DAILY SCHEDULE	PEOPLE TO CONTACT	THINGS TO DO
6:00am		
7:00am		
8:00am		
9:00am		
10:00am		
11:00am		
12:00 Noon		
1:00pm		
2:00pm		
3:00pm		
4:00pm		

DAILY SCHEDULE	ACTION TAKEN	GOAL	RESULT
5:00pm	PROSPECTS	3-10	
	CALLS	20-30	
6:00pm	INTERVIEWS	1-4	
	INVITES	2-5	
9:00pm	MEETINGS	2-3	
	RESULTS CATEGORY	RESULTS	
10:00pm	RECRUITS		
	SALES		
11:00pm	RESIDUALS		

PROSPECT GENERATION SHEET

M = Married   C = Children   H = Home Owner   FT = Full-Time Job

NAME	PHONE	NOTES (CIRCLE APPLICABLE)
1		M C H FT
2		M C H FT
3		M C H FT
4		M C H FT
5		M C H FT
6		M C H FT
7		M C H FT
8		M C H FT
9		M C H FT
10		M C H FT

PROSPECT GENERATION SHEET

M = Married   C = Children   H = Home Owner   FT = Full-Time Job

NAME	PHONE	NOTES (CIRCLE APPLICABLE)
1		M C H FT
2		M C H FT
3		M C H FT
4		M C H FT
5		M C H FT
6		M C H FT
7		M C H FT
8		M C H FT
9		M C H FT
10		M C H FT

FOLLOW UP SHEET

NAME	PHONE	NOTES

DAILY MASSIVE ACTION PLAN

Goals & Affirmations For Day	Time:	Date:

DAILY SCHEDULE	PEOPLE TO CONTACT	THINGS TO DO
6:00am		
7:00am		
8:00am		
9:00am		
10:00am		
11:00am		
12:00 Noon		
1:00pm		
2:00pm		
3:00pm		
4:00pm		

DAILY SCHEDULE	ACTION TAKEN	GOAL	RESULT
5:00pm	PROSPECTS	3-10	
6:00pm	CALLS	20-30	
	INTERVIEWS	1-4	
9:00pm	INVITES	2-5	
	MEETINGS	2-3	
10:00pm	RESULTS CATEGORY	RESULTS	
	RECRUITS		
11:00pm	SALES		
	RESIDUALS		

PROSPECT GENERATION SHEET

M = Married   C = Children   H = Home Owner   FT = Full-Time Job

NAME	PHONE	NOTES (CIRCLE APPLICABLE)
1		M C H FT
2		M C H FT
3		M C H FT
4		M C H FT
5		M C H FT
6		M C H FT
7		M C H FT
8		M C H FT
9		M C H FT
10		M C H FT

PROSPECT GENERATION SHEET

M = Married   C = Children   H = Home Owner   FT = Full-Time Job

NAME	PHONE	NOTES (CIRCLE APPLICABLE)	
1			M C H FT
2			M C H FT
3			M C H FT
4			M C H FT
5			M C H FT
6			M C H FT
7			M C H FT
8			M C H FT
9			M C H FT
10			M C H FT

FOLLOW UP SHEET

NAME	PHONE	NOTES

WEEKLY ACTIVITY LOG / WEEK OF: _____

Be the Most Productive Person You Can Be At All Times

	SUNDAY	MONDAY	TUESDAY	WEDNESDAY	THURSDAY	FRIDAY	SATURDAY
8am							
9am							
10am							
11am							
12 noon							
1pm							
2pm							
3pm							
4pm							
5pm							
6pm							
7pm							
8pm							
9pm							

Persistence:

"Firm or obstinate continuance in a course of action in spite of difficulty or opposition."

Massive Action Plan To Get $_____ / Yr. Income

Weekly Activity Planner For The Week Of: _____

WEEKLY	GOAL	SUN	MON	TUE	WED	THU	FRI	SAT
PROSPECTS	20							
CALLS	100							
INTERVIEWS	15							
INVITES	10							
MEETINGS	10							
SIGN UPS								
SALES	$							
RESIDUALS	$							

MTD #'s	RECRUITS	RESIDUALS	SALES
PERSONAL			
TEAM			

MEETINGS
1
2
3
4
5
6
7
8
9
10

INTERVIEWS
1
2
3
4
5
6
7
8
9
10

PROSPECTS
1
2
3
4
5
6
7
8

CALLS
1
2
3
4
5
6
7
8
9
10
11
12
13
14
15

DAILY MASSIVE ACTION PLAN

Goals & Affirmations For Day	Time:	Date:

DAILY SCHEDULE	PEOPLE TO CONTACT	THINGS TO DO
6:00am		
7:00am		
8:00am		
9:00am		
10:00am		
11:00am		
12:00 Noon		
1:00pm		
2:00pm		
3:00pm		
4:00pm		

DAILY SCHEDULE	ACTION TAKEN	GOAL	RESULT
5:00pm	PROSPECTS	3-10	
6:00pm	CALLS	20-30	
	INTERVIEWS	1-4	
9:00pm	INVITES	2-5	
	MEETINGS	2-3	

DAILY SCHEDULE	RESULTS CATEGORY	RESULTS	
10:00pm	RECRUITS		
11:00pm	SALES		
	RESIDUALS		

PROSPECT GENERATION SHEET

M = Married   C = Children   H = Home Owner   FT = Full-Time Job

NAME	PHONE	NOTES (CIRCLE APPLICABLE)	
1			M C H FT
2			M C H FT
3			M C H FT
4			M C H FT
5			M C H FT
6			M C H FT
7			M C H FT
8			M C H FT
9			M C H FT
10			M C H FT

PROSPECT GENERATION SHEET

M = Married   C = Children   H = Home Owner   FT = Full-Time Job

NAME	PHONE	NOTES (CIRCLE APPLICABLE)	
1			M C H FT
2			M C H FT
3			M C H FT
4			M C H FT
5			M C H FT
6			M C H FT
7			M C H FT
8			M C H FT
9			M C H FT
10			M C H FT

FOLLOW UP SHEET

NAME	PHONE	NOTES

DAILY MASSIVE ACTION PLAN

Goals & Affirmations For Day	Time:	Date:

DAILY SCHEDULE	PEOPLE TO CONTACT	THINGS TO DO
6:00am		
7:00am		
8:00am		
9:00am		
10:00am		
11:00am		
12:00 Noon		
1:00pm		
2:00pm		
3:00pm		
4:00pm		

DAILY SCHEDULE	ACTION TAKEN	GOAL	RESULT
5:00pm	PROSPECTS	3-10	
6:00pm	CALLS	20-30	
	INTERVIEWS	1-4	
9:00pm	INVITES	2-5	
	MEETINGS	2-3	

	RESULTS CATEGORY	RESULTS	
10:00pm	RECRUITS		
11:00pm	SALES		
	RESIDUALS		

PROSPECT GENERATION SHEET

M = Married   C = Children   H = Home Owner   FT = Full-Time Job

NAME	PHONE	NOTES (CIRCLE APPLICABLE)	
1			M C H FT
2			M C H FT
3			M C H FT
4			M C H FT
5			M C H FT
6			M C H FT
7			M C H FT
8			M C H FT
9			M C H FT
10			M C H FT

PROSPECT GENERATION SHEET

M = Married   C = Children   H = Home Owner   FT = Full-Time Job

NAME	PHONE	NOTES (CIRCLE APPLICABLE)	
1			M C H FT
2			M C H FT
3			M C H FT
4			M C H FT
5			M C H FT
6			M C H FT
7			M C H FT
8			M C H FT
9			M C H FT
10			M C H FT

FOLLOW UP SHEET

NAME	PHONE	NOTES

DAILY MASSIVE ACTION PLAN

Goals & Affirmations For Day	Time:	Date:	

DAILY SCHEDULE	PEOPLE TO CONTACT	THINGS TO DO
6:00am		
7:00am		
8:00am		
9:00am		
10:00am		
11:00am		
12:00 Noon		
1:00pm		
2:00pm		
3:00pm		
4:00pm		

DAILY SCHEDULE	ACTION TAKEN	GOAL	RESULT
5:00pm	PROSPECTS	3-10	
6:00pm	CALLS	20-30	
	INTERVIEWS	1-4	
9:00pm	INVITES	2-5	
	MEETINGS	2-3	
10:00pm	RESULTS CATEGORY	RESULTS	
	RECRUITS		
11:00pm	SALES		
	RESIDUALS		

PROSPECT GENERATION SHEET

M = Married   C = Children   H = Home Owner   FT = Full-Time Job

NAME	PHONE	NOTES (CIRCLE APPLICABLE)	
1			M C H FT
2			M C H FT
3			M C H FT
4			M C H FT
5			M C H FT
6			M C H FT
7			M C H FT
8			M C H FT
9			M C H FT
10			M C H FT

PROSPECT GENERATION SHEET

M = Married   C = Children   H = Home Owner   FT = Full-Time Job

NAME	PHONE	NOTES (CIRCLE APPLICABLE)
1		M C H FT
2		M C H FT
3		M C H FT
4		M C H FT
5		M C H FT
6		M C H FT
7		M C H FT
8		M C H FT
9		M C H FT
10		M C H FT

FOLLOW UP SHEET

NAME	PHONE	NOTES

DAILY MASSIVE ACTION PLAN

Goals & Affirmations For Day	Time:	Date:

DAILY SCHEDULE	PEOPLE TO CONTACT	THINGS TO DO
6:00am		
7:00am		
8:00am		
9:00am		
10:00am		
11:00am		
12:00 Noon		
1:00pm		
2:00pm		
3:00pm		
4:00pm		

DAILY SCHEDULE	ACTION TAKEN	GOAL	RESULT
5:00pm	PROSPECTS	3-10	
6:00pm	CALLS	20-30	
	INTERVIEWS	1-4	
9:00pm	INVITES	2-5	
	MEETINGS	2-3	
10:00pm	RESULTS CATEGORY	RESULTS	
	RECRUITS		
11:00pm	SALES		
	RESIDUALS		

PROSPECT GENERATION SHEET

M = Married   C = Children   H = Home Owner   FT = Full-Time Job

NAME	PHONE	NOTES (CIRCLE APPLICABLE)	
1			M C H FT
2			M C H FT
3			M C H FT
4			M C H FT
5			M C H FT
6			M C H FT
7			M C H FT
8			M C H FT
9			M C H FT
10			M C H FT

PROSPECT GENERATION SHEET

M = Married   C = Children   H = Home Owner   FT = Full-Time Job

NAME	PHONE	NOTES (CIRCLE APPLICABLE)
1		M C H FT
2		M C H FT
3		M C H FT
4		M C H FT
5		M C H FT
6		M C H FT
7		M C H FT
8		M C H FT
9		M C H FT
10		M C H FT

FOLLOW UP SHEET

NAME	PHONE	NOTES

DAILY MASSIVE ACTION PLAN

Goals & Affirmations For Day	Time:	Date:

DAILY SCHEDULE	PEOPLE TO CONTACT	THINGS TO DO
6:00am		
7:00am		
8:00am		
9:00am		
10:00am		
11:00am		
12:00 Noon		
1:00pm		
2:00pm		
3:00pm		
4:00pm		

DAILY SCHEDULE	ACTION TAKEN	GOAL	RESULT
5:00pm	PROSPECTS	3-10	
6:00pm	CALLS	20-30	
	INTERVIEWS	1-4	
9:00pm	INVITES	2-5	
	MEETINGS	2-3	
10:00pm	RESULTS CATEGORY	RESULTS	
	RECRUITS		
11:00pm	SALES		
	RESIDUALS		

PROSPECT GENERATION SHEET

M = Married   C = Children   H = Home Owner   FT = Full-Time Job

	NAME	PHONE	NOTES (CIRCLE APPLICABLE)
1			M C H FT
2			M C H FT
3			M C H FT
4			M C H FT
5			M C H FT
6			M C H FT
7			M C H FT
8			M C H FT
9			M C H FT
10			M C H FT

PROSPECT GENERATION SHEET

M = Married   C = Children   H = Home Owner   FT = Full-Time Job

NAME	PHONE	NOTES (CIRCLE APPLICABLE)
1		M C H FT
2		M C H FT
3		M C H FT
4		M C H FT
5		M C H FT
6		M C H FT
7		M C H FT
8		M C H FT
9		M C H FT
10		M C H FT

FOLLOW UP SHEET

NAME	PHONE	NOTES

DAILY MASSIVE ACTION PLAN

Goals & Affirmations For Day	Time:	Date:

DAILY SCHEDULE	PEOPLE TO CONTACT	THINGS TO DO
6:00am		
7:00am		
8:00am		
9:00am		
10:00am		
11:00am		
12:00 Noon		
1:00pm		
2:00pm		
3:00pm		
4:00pm		

	ACTION TAKEN	GOAL	RESULT
5:00pm	PROSPECTS	3-10	
6:00pm	CALLS	20-30	
	INTERVIEWS	1-4	
9:00pm	INVITES	2-5	
	MEETINGS	2-3	

	RESULTS CATEGORY	RESULTS
10:00pm	RECRUITS	
11:00pm	SALES	
	RESIDUALS	

PROSPECT GENERATION SHEET

M = Married   C = Children   H = Home Owner   FT = Full-Time Job

NAME	PHONE	NOTES (CIRCLE APPLICABLE)	
1			M C H FT
2			M C H FT
3			M C H FT
4			M C H FT
5			M C H FT
6			M C H FT
7			M C H FT
8			M C H FT
9			M C H FT
10			M C H FT

PROSPECT GENERATION SHEET

M = Married   C = Children   H = Home Owner   FT = Full-Time Job

NAME	PHONE	NOTES (CIRCLE APPLICABLE)
1		M C H FT
2		M C H FT
3		M C H FT
4		M C H FT
5		M C H FT
6		M C H FT
7		M C H FT
8		M C H FT
9		M C H FT
10		M C H FT

FOLLOW UP SHEET

NAME	PHONE	NOTES

DAILY MASSIVE ACTION PLAN

Goals & Affirmations For Day	Time:	Date:

DAILY SCHEDULE	PEOPLE TO CONTACT	THINGS TO DO
6:00am		
7:00am		
8:00am		
9:00am		
10:00am		
11:00am		
12:00 Noon		
1:00pm		
2:00pm		
3:00pm		
4:00pm		

DAILY SCHEDULE	ACTION TAKEN	GOAL	RESULT
5:00pm	PROSPECTS	3-10	
6:00pm	CALLS	20-30	
	INTERVIEWS	1-4	
9:00pm	INVITES	2-5	
	MEETINGS	2-3	
10:00pm	RESULTS CATEGORY	RESULTS	
	RECRUITS		
11:00pm	SALES		
	RESIDUALS		

PROSPECT GENERATION SHEET

M = Married   C = Children   H = Home Owner   FT = Full-Time Job

NAME	PHONE	NOTES (CIRCLE APPLICABLE)	
1			M C H FT
2			M C H FT
3			M C H FT
4			M C H FT
5			M C H FT
6			M C H FT
7			M C H FT
8			M C H FT
9			M C H FT
10			M C H FT

PROSPECT GENERATION SHEET

M = Married   C = Children   H = Home Owner   FT = Full-Time Job

NAME	PHONE	NOTES (CIRCLE APPLICABLE)	
1			M C H FT
2			M C H FT
3			M C H FT
4			M C H FT
5			M C H FT
6			M C H FT
7			M C H FT
8			M C H FT
9			M C H FT
10			M C H FT

FOLLOW UP SHEET

NAME	PHONE	NOTES

WEEKLY ACTIVITY LOG / WEEK OF: _____

Be the Most Productive Person You Can Be At All Times

	SUNDAY	MONDAY	TUESDAY	WEDNESDAY	THURSDAY	FRIDAY	SATURDAY
8am							
9am							
10am							
11am							
12 noon							
1pm							
2pm							
3pm							
4pm							
5pm							
6pm							
7pm							
8pm							
9pm							

Persistence:

"Firm or obstinate continuance in a course of action in spite of difficulty or opposition."

Massive Action Plan To Get $_____ / Yr. Income

Weekly Activity Planner For The Week Of: _____

WEEKLY	GOAL	SUN	MON	TUE	WED	THU	FRI	SAT
PROSPECTS	20							
CALLS	100							
INTERVIEWS	15							
INVITES	10							
MEETINGS	10							
SIGN UPS								
SALES	$							
RESIDUALS	$							

MTD #'s	RECRUITS	RESIDUALS	SALES
PERSONAL			
TEAM			

MEETINGS

1	
2	
3	
4	
5	
6	
7	
8	
9	
10	

INTERVIEWS

1	
2	
3	
4	
5	
6	
7	
8	
9	
10	

PROSPECTS

1	
2	
3	
4	
5	
6	
7	
8	

CALLS

1	
2	
3	
4	
5	
6	
7	
8	
9	
10	
11	
12	
13	
14	
15	

DAILY MASSIVE ACTION PLAN

Goals & Affirmations For Day	Time:	Date:

DAILY SCHEDULE	PEOPLE TO CONTACT	THINGS TO DO
6:00am		
7:00am		
8:00am		
9:00am		
10:00am		
11:00am		
12:00 Noon		
1:00pm		
2:00pm		
3:00pm		
4:00pm		

DAILY SCHEDULE	ACTION TAKEN	GOAL	RESULT
5:00pm	PROSPECTS	3-10	
6:00pm	CALLS	20-30	
	INTERVIEWS	1-4	
9:00pm	INVITES	2-5	
	MEETINGS	2-3	

	RESULTS CATEGORY	RESULTS	
10:00pm	RECRUITS		
	SALES		
11:00pm	RESIDUALS		

PROSPECT GENERATION SHEET

M = Married   C = Children   H = Home Owner   FT = Full-Time Job

NAME	PHONE	NOTES (CIRCLE APPLICABLE)
1		M C H FT
2		M C H FT
3		M C H FT
4		M C H FT
5		M C H FT
6		M C H FT
7		M C H FT
8		M C H FT
9		M C H FT
10		M C H FT

PROSPECT GENERATION SHEET

M = Married   C = Children   H = Home Owner   FT = Full-Time Job

NAME	PHONE	NOTES (CIRCLE APPLICABLE)
1		M C H FT
2		M C H FT
3		M C H FT
4		M C H FT
5		M C H FT
6		M C H FT
7		M C H FT
8		M C H FT
9		M C H FT
10		M C H FT

FOLLOW UP SHEET

NAME	PHONE	NOTES

DAILY MASSIVE ACTION PLAN

Goals & Affirmations For Day	Time:	Date:

DAILY SCHEDULE	PEOPLE TO CONTACT	THINGS TO DO
6:00am		
7:00am		
8:00am		
9:00am		
10:00am		
11:00am		
12:00 Noon		
1:00pm		
2:00pm		
3:00pm		
4:00pm		

	ACTION TAKEN	GOAL	RESULT
5:00pm	PROSPECTS	3-10	
6:00pm	CALLS	20-30	
	INTERVIEWS	1-4	
9:00pm	INVITES	2-5	
	MEETINGS	2-3	

	RESULTS CATEGORY	RESULTS
10:00pm	RECRUITS	
11:00pm	SALES	
	RESIDUALS	

PROSPECT GENERATION SHEET

M = Married   C = Children   H = Home Owner   FT = Full-Time Job

NAME	PHONE	NOTES (CIRCLE APPLICABLE)	
1			M C H FT
2			M C H FT
3			M C H FT
4			M C H FT
5			M C H FT
6			M C H FT
7			M C H FT
8			M C H FT
9			M C H FT
10			M C H FT

PROSPECT GENERATION SHEET

M = Married   C = Children   H = Home Owner   FT = Full-Time Job

NAME	PHONE	NOTES (CIRCLE APPLICABLE)	
1			M C H FT
2			M C H FT
3			M C H FT
4			M C H FT
5			M C H FT
6			M C H FT
7			M C H FT
8			M C H FT
9			M C H FT
10			M C H FT

FOLLOW UP SHEET

NAME	PHONE	NOTES

DAILY MASSIVE ACTION PLAN

Goals & Affirmations For Day	Time:	Date:

DAILY SCHEDULE	PEOPLE TO CONTACT	THINGS TO DO
6:00am		
7:00am		
8:00am		
9:00am		
10:00am		
11:00am		
12:00 Noon		
1:00pm		
2:00pm		
3:00pm		
4:00pm		
5:00pm		

ACTION TAKEN	GOAL	RESULT
PROSPECTS	3-10	
CALLS	20-30	
INTERVIEWS	1-4	
INVITES	2-5	
MEETINGS	2-3	

RESULTS CATEGORY	RESULTS	
RECRUITS		
SALES		
RESIDUALS		

PROSPECT GENERATION SHEET

M = Married   C = Children   H = Home Owner   FT = Full-Time Job

NAME	PHONE	NOTES (CIRCLE APPLICABLE)	
1			M C H FT
2			M C H FT
3			M C H FT
4			M C H FT
5			M C H FT
6			M C H FT
7			M C H FT
8			M C H FT
9			M C H FT
10			M C H FT

PROSPECT GENERATION SHEET

M = Married   C = Children   H = Home Owner   FT = Full-Time Job

NAME	PHONE	NOTES (CIRCLE APPLICABLE)
1		M C H FT
2		M C H FT
3		M C H FT
4		M C H FT
5		M C H FT
6		M C H FT
7		M C H FT
8		M C H FT
9		M C H FT
10		M C H FT

FOLLOW UP SHEET

NAME	PHONE	NOTES

DAILY MASSIVE ACTION PLAN

Goals & Affirmations For Day	Time:	Date:

DAILY SCHEDULE	PEOPLE TO CONTACT	THINGS TO DO
6:00am		
7:00am		
8:00am		
9:00am		
10:00am		
11:00am		
12:00 Noon		
1:00pm		
2:00pm		
3:00pm		
4:00pm		

DAILY SCHEDULE	ACTION TAKEN	GOAL	RESULT
5:00pm	PROSPECTS	3-10	
6:00pm	CALLS	20-30	
	INTERVIEWS	1-4	
9:00pm	INVITES	2-5	
	MEETINGS	2-3	
10:00pm	RESULTS CATEGORY	RESULTS	
	RECRUITS		
11:00pm	SALES		
	RESIDUALS		

PROSPECT GENERATION SHEET

M = Married   C = Children   H = Home Owner   FT = Full-Time Job

NAME	PHONE	NOTES (CIRCLE APPLICABLE)	
1			M C H FT
2			M C H FT
3			M C H FT
4			M C H FT
5			M C H FT
6			M C H FT
7			M C H FT
8			M C H FT
9			M C H FT
10			M C H FT

PROSPECT GENERATION SHEET

M = Married   C = Children   H = Home Owner   FT = Full-Time Job

NAME	PHONE	NOTES (CIRCLE APPLICABLE)
1		M C H FT
2		M C H FT
3		M C H FT
4		M C H FT
5		M C H FT
6		M C H FT
7		M C H FT
8		M C H FT
9		M C H FT
10		M C H FT

FOLLOW UP SHEET

NAME	PHONE	NOTES

DAILY MASSIVE ACTION PLAN

Goals & Affirmations For Day	Time:	Date:

DAILY SCHEDULE	PEOPLE TO CONTACT	THINGS TO DO
6:00am		
7:00am		
8:00am		
9:00am		
10:00am		
11:00am		
12:00 Noon		
1:00pm		
2:00pm		
3:00pm		
4:00pm		

DAILY SCHEDULE	ACTION TAKEN	GOAL	RESULT
5:00pm	PROSPECTS	3-10	
6:00pm	CALLS	20-30	
	INTERVIEWS	1-4	
9:00pm	INVITES	2-5	
	MEETINGS	2-3	
10:00pm	RESULTS CATEGORY	RESULTS	
	RECRUITS		
11:00pm	SALES		
	RESIDUALS		

PROSPECT GENERATION SHEET

M = Married   C = Children   H = Home Owner   FT = Full-Time Job

NAME	PHONE	NOTES (CIRCLE APPLICABLE)	
1			M C H FT
2			M C H FT
3			M C H FT
4			M C H FT
5			M C H FT
6			M C H FT
7			M C H FT
8			M C H FT
9			M C H FT
10			M C H FT

PROSPECT GENERATION SHEET

M = Married   C = Children   H = Home Owner   FT = Full-Time Job

NAME	PHONE	NOTES (CIRCLE APPLICABLE)
1		M C H FT
2		M C H FT
3		M C H FT
4		M C H FT
5		M C H FT
6		M C H FT
7		M C H FT
8		M C H FT
9		M C H FT
10		M C H FT

FOLLOW UP SHEET

NAME	PHONE	NOTES

DAILY MASSIVE ACTION PLAN

Goals & Affirmations For Day	Time:	Date:

DAILY SCHEDULE	PEOPLE TO CONTACT	THINGS TO DO
6:00am		
7:00am		
8:00am		
9:00am		
10:00am		
11:00am		
12:00 Noon		
1:00pm		
2:00pm		
3:00pm		
4:00pm		

DAILY SCHEDULE	ACTION TAKEN	GOAL	RESULT
5:00pm	PROSPECTS	3-10	
6:00pm	CALLS	20-30	
	INTERVIEWS	1-4	
9:00pm	INVITES	2-5	
	MEETINGS	2-3	
10:00pm	RESULTS CATEGORY	RESULTS	
	RECRUITS		
11:00pm	SALES		
	RESIDUALS		

PROSPECT GENERATION SHEET

M = Married   C = Children   H = Home Owner   FT = Full-Time Job

NAME	PHONE	NOTES (CIRCLE APPLICABLE)
1		M C H FT
2		M C H FT
3		M C H FT
4		M C H FT
5		M C H FT
6		M C H FT
7		M C H FT
8		M C H FT
9		M C H FT
10		M C H FT

PROSPECT GENERATION SHEET

M = Married   C = Children   H = Home Owner   FT = Full-Time Job

NAME	PHONE	NOTES (CIRCLE APPLICABLE)
1		M C H FT
2		M C H FT
3		M C H FT
4		M C H FT
5		M C H FT
6		M C H FT
7		M C H FT
8		M C H FT
9		M C H FT
10		M C H FT

FOLLOW UP SHEET

NAME	PHONE	NOTES

DAILY MASSIVE ACTION PLAN

Goals & Affirmations For Day		Time:		Date:	

DAILY SCHEDULE	PEOPLE TO CONTACT	THINGS TO DO
6:00am		
7:00am		
8:00am		
9:00am		
10:00am		
11:00am		
12:00 Noon		
1:00pm		
2:00pm		
3:00pm		
4:00pm		

DAILY SCHEDULE	ACTION TAKEN	GOAL	RESULT
5:00pm	PROSPECTS	3-10	
6:00pm	CALLS	20-30	
	INTERVIEWS	1-4	
9:00pm	INVITES	2-5	
	MEETINGS	2-3	
10:00pm	RESULTS CATEGORY	RESULTS	
	RECRUITS		
11:00pm	SALES		
	RESIDUALS		

PROSPECT GENERATION SHEET

M = Married   C = Children   H = Home Owner   FT = Full-Time Job

NAME	PHONE	NOTES (CIRCLE APPLICABLE)
1		M C H FT
2		M C H FT
3		M C H FT
4		M C H FT
5		M C H FT
6		M C H FT
7		M C H FT
8		M C H FT
9		M C H FT
10		M C H FT

PROSPECT GENERATION SHEET

M = Married   C = Children   H = Home Owner   FT = Full-Time Job

NAME	PHONE	NOTES (CIRCLE APPLICABLE)	
1			M C H FT
2			M C H FT
3			M C H FT
4			M C H FT
5			M C H FT
6			M C H FT
7			M C H FT
8			M C H FT
9			M C H FT
10			M C H FT

FOLLOW UP SHEET

NAME	PHONE	NOTES

WEEKLY ACTIVITY LOG / WEEK OF: _____

Be the Most Productive Person You Can Be At All Times

	SUNDAY	MONDAY	TUESDAY	WEDNESDAY	THURSDAY	FRIDAY	SATURDAY
8am							
9am							
10am							
11am							
12 noon							
1pm							
2pm							
3pm							
4pm							
5pm							
6pm							
7pm							
8pm							
9pm							

Persistence:

"Firm or obstinate continuance in a course of action in spite of difficulty or opposition."

Massive Action Plan To Get $_____ / Yr. Income
Weekly Activity Planner For The Week Of: _____

WEEKLY	GOAL	SUN	MON	TUE	WED	THU	FRI	SAT
PROSPECTS	20							
CALLS	100							
INTERVIEWS	15							
INVITES	10							
MEETINGS	10							
SIGN UPS								
SALES	$							
RESIDUALS	$							

MTD #'s	RECRUITS	RESIDUALS	SALES
PERSONAL			
TEAM			

PROSPECTS
1	
2	
3	
4	
5	
6	
7	
8	

MEETINGS
1	
2	
3	
4	
5	
6	
7	
8	
9	
10	

CALLS
1	
2	
3	
4	
5	
6	
7	
8	
9	
10	
11	
12	
13	
14	
15	

INTERVIEWS
1	
2	
3	
4	
5	
6	
7	
8	
9	
10	

DAILY MASSIVE ACTION PLAN

Goals & Affirmations For Day	Time:	Date:

DAILY SCHEDULE	PEOPLE TO CONTACT	THINGS TO DO
6:00am		
7:00am		
8:00am		
9:00am		
10:00am		
11:00am		
12:00 Noon		
1:00pm		
2:00pm		
3:00pm		
4:00pm		

DAILY SCHEDULE	ACTION TAKEN	GOAL	RESULT
5:00pm	PROSPECTS	3-10	
6:00pm	CALLS	20-30	
	INTERVIEWS	1-4	
9:00pm	INVITES	2-5	
	MEETINGS	2-3	
10:00pm	RESULTS CATEGORY	RESULTS	
	RECRUITS		
11:00pm	SALES		
	RESIDUALS		

PROSPECT GENERATION SHEET

M = Married   C = Children   H = Home Owner   FT = Full-Time Job

NAME	PHONE	NOTES (CIRCLE APPLICABLE)	
1			M C H FT
2			M C H FT
3			M C H FT
4			M C H FT
5			M C H FT
6			M C H FT
7			M C H FT
8			M C H FT
9			M C H FT
10			M C H FT

PROSPECT GENERATION SHEET

M = Married   C = Children   H = Home Owner   FT = Full-Time Job

NAME	PHONE	NOTES (CIRCLE APPLICABLE)	
1			M C H FT
2			M C H FT
3			M C H FT
4			M C H FT
5			M C H FT
6			M C H FT
7			M C H FT
8			M C H FT
9			M C H FT
10			M C H FT

FOLLOW UP SHEET

NAME	PHONE	NOTES

DAILY MASSIVE ACTION PLAN

Goals & Affirmations For Day	Time:	Date:	

DAILY SCHEDULE	PEOPLE TO CONTACT	THINGS TO DO
6:00am		
7:00am		
8:00am		
9:00am		
10:00am		
11:00am		
12:00 Noon		
1:00pm		
2:00pm		
3:00pm		
4:00pm		
5:00pm		

	ACTION TAKEN	GOAL	RESULT
5:00pm	PROSPECTS	3-10	
6:00pm	CALLS	20-30	
	INTERVIEWS	1-4	
9:00pm	INVITES	2-5	
	MEETINGS	2-3	
10:00pm	RESULTS CATEGORY	RESULTS	
	RECRUITS		
11:00pm	SALES		
	RESIDUALS		

PROSPECT GENERATION SHEET

M = Married   C = Children   H = Home Owner   FT = Full-Time Job

NAME	PHONE	NOTES (CIRCLE APPLICABLE)	
1			M C H FT
2			M C H FT
3			M C H FT
4			M C H FT
5			M C H FT
6			M C H FT
7			M C H FT
8			M C H FT
9			M C H FT
10			M C H FT

PROSPECT GENERATION SHEET

M = Married   C = Children   H = Home Owner   FT = Full-Time Job

NAME	PHONE	NOTES (CIRCLE APPLICABLE)
1		M C H FT
2		M C H FT
3		M C H FT
4		M C H FT
5		M C H FT
6		M C H FT
7		M C H FT
8		M C H FT
9		M C H FT
10		M C H FT

FOLLOW UP SHEET

NAME	PHONE	NOTES

DAILY MASSIVE ACTION PLAN

Goals & Affirmations For Day	Time:	Date:

DAILY SCHEDULE	PEOPLE TO CONTACT	THINGS TO DO
6:00am		
7:00am		
8:00am		
9:00am		
10:00am		
11:00am		
12:00 Noon		
1:00pm		
2:00pm		
3:00pm		
4:00pm		

	ACTION TAKEN	GOAL	RESULT
5:00pm	PROSPECTS	3-10	
6:00pm	CALLS	20-30	
	INTERVIEWS	1-4	
9:00pm	INVITES	2-5	
	MEETINGS	2-3	

	RESULTS CATEGORY	RESULTS
10:00pm	RECRUITS	
11:00pm	SALES	
	RESIDUALS	

PROSPECT GENERATION SHEET

M = Married   C = Children   H = Home Owner   FT = Full-Time Job

NAME	PHONE	NOTES (CIRCLE APPLICABLE)	
1			M C H FT
2			M C H FT
3			M C H FT
4			M C H FT
5			M C H FT
6			M C H FT
7			M C H FT
8			M C H FT
9			M C H FT
10			M C H FT

PROSPECT GENERATION SHEET

M = Married   C = Children   H = Home Owner   FT = Full-Time Job

NAME	PHONE	NOTES (CIRCLE APPLICABLE)	
1			M C H FT
2			M C H FT
3			M C H FT
4			M C H FT
5			M C H FT
6			M C H FT
7			M C H FT
8			M C H FT
9			M C H FT
10			M C H FT

FOLLOW UP SHEET

NAME	PHONE	NOTES

DAILY MASSIVE ACTION PLAN

Goals & Affirmations For Day	Time:	Date:

DAILY SCHEDULE	PEOPLE TO CONTACT	THINGS TO DO
6:00am		
7:00am		
8:00am		
9:00am		
10:00am		
11:00am		
12:00 Noon		
1:00pm		
2:00pm		
3:00pm		
4:00pm		

DAILY SCHEDULE	ACTION TAKEN	GOAL	RESULT
5:00pm	PROSPECTS	3-10	
6:00pm	CALLS	20-30	
	INTERVIEWS	1-4	
9:00pm	INVITES	2-5	
	MEETINGS	2-3	
10:00pm	RESULTS CATEGORY	RESULTS	
	RECRUITS		
11:00pm	SALES		
	RESIDUALS		

PROSPECT GENERATION SHEET

M = Married   C = Children   H = Home Owner   FT = Full-Time Job

NAME	PHONE	NOTES (CIRCLE APPLICABLE)
1		M C H FT
2		M C H FT
3		M C H FT
4		M C H FT
5		M C H FT
6		M C H FT
7		M C H FT
8		M C H FT
9		M C H FT
10		M C H FT

PROSPECT GENERATION SHEET

M = Married   C = Children   H = Home Owner   FT = Full-Time Job

NAME	PHONE	NOTES (CIRCLE APPLICABLE)	
1			M C H FT
2			M C H FT
3			M C H FT
4			M C H FT
5			M C H FT
6			M C H FT
7			M C H FT
8			M C H FT
9			M C H FT
10			M C H FT

FOLLOW UP SHEET

NAME	PHONE	NOTES

DAILY MASSIVE ACTION PLAN

Goals & Affirmations For Day	Time:	Date:

DAILY SCHEDULE	PEOPLE TO CONTACT	THINGS TO DO
6:00am		
7:00am		
8:00am		
9:00am		
10:00am		
11:00am		
12:00 Noon		
1:00pm		
2:00pm		
3:00pm		
4:00pm		

DAILY SCHEDULE	ACTION TAKEN	GOAL	RESULT
5:00pm	PROSPECTS	3-10	
6:00pm	CALLS	20-30	
	INTERVIEWS	1-4	
9:00pm	INVITES	2-5	
	MEETINGS	2-3	
10:00pm	RESULTS CATEGORY	RESULTS	
	RECRUITS		
11:00pm	SALES		
	RESIDUALS		

PROSPECT GENERATION SHEET

M = Married   C = Children   H = Home Owner   FT = Full-Time Job

NAME	PHONE	NOTES (CIRCLE APPLICABLE)	
1			M C H FT
2			M C H FT
3			M C H FT
4			M C H FT
5			M C H FT
6			M C H FT
7			M C H FT
8			M C H FT
9			M C H FT
10			M C H FT

PROSPECT GENERATION SHEET

M = Married   C = Children   H = Home Owner   FT = Full-Time Job

NAME	PHONE	NOTES (CIRCLE APPLICABLE)
1		M C H FT
2		M C H FT
3		M C H FT
4		M C H FT
5		M C H FT
6		M C H FT
7		M C H FT
8		M C H FT
9		M C H FT
10		M C H FT

FOLLOW UP SHEET

NAME	PHONE	NOTES

DAILY MASSIVE ACTION PLAN

Goals & Affirmations For Day	Time:	Date:

DAILY SCHEDULE	PEOPLE TO CONTACT	THINGS TO DO
6:00am		
7:00am		
8:00am		
9:00am		
10:00am		
11:00am		
12:00 Noon		
1:00pm		
2:00pm		
3:00pm		
4:00pm		

DAILY SCHEDULE	ACTION TAKEN	GOAL	RESULT
5:00pm	PROSPECTS	3-10	
6:00pm	CALLS	20-30	
	INTERVIEWS	1-4	
9:00pm	INVITES	2-5	
	MEETINGS	2-3	

DAILY SCHEDULE	RESULTS CATEGORY	RESULTS	
10:00pm	RECRUITS		
11:00pm	SALES		
	RESIDUALS		

PROSPECT GENERATION SHEET

M = Married   C = Children   H = Home Owner   FT = Full-Time Job

NAME	PHONE	NOTES (CIRCLE APPLICABLE)
1		M C H FT
2		M C H FT
3		M C H FT
4		M C H FT
5		M C H FT
6		M C H FT
7		M C H FT
8		M C H FT
9		M C H FT
10		M C H FT

PROSPECT GENERATION SHEET

M = Married   C = Children   H = Home Owner   FT = Full-Time Job

NAME	PHONE	NOTES (CIRCLE APPLICABLE)
1		M C H FT
2		M C H FT
3		M C H FT
4		M C H FT
5		M C H FT
6		M C H FT
7		M C H FT
8		M C H FT
9		M C H FT
10		M C H FT

FOLLOW UP SHEET

NAME	PHONE	NOTES

DAILY MASSIVE ACTION PLAN

Goals & Affirmations For Day	Time:	Date:

DAILY SCHEDULE	PEOPLE TO CONTACT	THINGS TO DO
6:00am		
7:00am		
8:00am		
9:00am		
10:00am		
11:00am		
12:00 Noon		
1:00pm		
2:00pm		
3:00pm		
4:00pm		

DAILY SCHEDULE	ACTION TAKEN	GOAL	RESULT
5:00pm	PROSPECTS	3-10	
	CALLS	20-30	
6:00pm	INTERVIEWS	1-4	
	INVITES	2-5	
9:00pm	MEETINGS	2-3	

	RESULTS CATEGORY	RESULTS	
10:00pm	RECRUITS		
11:00pm	SALES		
	RESIDUALS		

PROSPECT GENERATION SHEET

M = Married   C = Children   H = Home Owner   FT = Full-Time Job

NAME	PHONE	NOTES (CIRCLE APPLICABLE)	
1			M C H FT
2			M C H FT
3			M C H FT
4			M C H FT
5			M C H FT
6			M C H FT
7			M C H FT
8			M C H FT
9			M C H FT
10			M C H FT

PROSPECT GENERATION SHEET

M = Married   C = Children   H = Home Owner   FT = Full-Time Job

NAME	PHONE	NOTES (CIRCLE APPLICABLE)
1		M C H FT
2		M C H FT
3		M C H FT
4		M C H FT
5		M C H FT
6		M C H FT
7		M C H FT
8		M C H FT
9		M C H FT
10		M C H FT

FOLLOW UP SHEET

NAME	PHONE	NOTES

WEEKLY ACTIVITY LOG / WEEK OF: _____

Be the Most Productive Person You Can Be At All Times

	SUNDAY	MONDAY	TUESDAY	WEDNESDAY	THURSDAY	FRIDAY	SATURDAY
8am							
9am							
10am							
11am							
12 noon							
1pm							
2pm							
3pm							
4pm							
5pm							
6pm							
7pm							
8pm							
9pm							

Persistence:

"Firm or obstinate continuance in a course of action in spite of difficulty or opposition."

Massive Action Plan To Get $_____ / Yr. Income

Weekly Activity Planner For The Week Of: _____

WEEKLY	GOAL	SUN	MON	TUE	WED	THU	FRI	SAT
PROSPECTS	20							
CALLS	100							
INTERVIEWS	15							
INVITES	10							
MEETINGS	10							
SIGN UPS								
SALES	$							
RESIDUALS	$							

MTD #'s	RECRUITS	RESIDUALS	SALES
PERSONAL			
TEAM			

MEETINGS
1
2
3
4
5
6
7
8
9
10

PROSPECTS
1
2
3
4
5
6
7
8

INTERVIEWS
1
2
3
4
5
6
7
8
9
10

CALLS
1
2
3
4
5
6
7
8
9
10
11
12
13
14
15

DAILY MASSIVE ACTION PLAN

Goals & Affirmations For Day	Time:	Date:

DAILY SCHEDULE	PEOPLE TO CONTACT	THINGS TO DO
6:00am		
7:00am		
8:00am		
9:00am		
10:00am		
11:00am		
12:00 Noon		
1:00pm		
2:00pm		
3:00pm		
4:00pm		

DAILY SCHEDULE	ACTION TAKEN	GOAL	RESULT
5:00pm	PROSPECTS	3-10	
6:00pm	CALLS	20-30	
	INTERVIEWS	1-4	
9:00pm	INVITES	2-5	
	MEETINGS	2-3	

DAILY SCHEDULE	RESULTS CATEGORY	RESULTS	
10:00pm	RECRUITS		
11:00pm	SALES		
	RESIDUALS		

PROSPECT GENERATION SHEET

M = Married   C = Children   H = Home Owner   FT = Full-Time Job

NAME	PHONE	NOTES (CIRCLE APPLICABLE)	
1			M C H FT
2			M C H FT
3			M C H FT
4			M C H FT
5			M C H FT
6			M C H FT
7			M C H FT
8			M C H FT
9			M C H FT
10			M C H FT

PROSPECT GENERATION SHEET

M = Married   C = Children   H = Home Owner   FT = Full-Time Job

NAME	PHONE	NOTES (CIRCLE APPLICABLE)	
1			M C H FT
2			M C H FT
3			M C H FT
4			M C H FT
5			M C H FT
6			M C H FT
7			M C H FT
8			M C H FT
9			M C H FT
10			M C H FT

FOLLOW UP SHEET

NAME	PHONE	NOTES

DAILY MASSIVE ACTION PLAN

Goals & Affirmations For Day	Time:	Date:

DAILY SCHEDULE	PEOPLE TO CONTACT	THINGS TO DO
6:00am		
7:00am		
8:00am		
9:00am		
10:00am		
11:00am		
12:00 Noon		
1:00pm		
2:00pm		
3:00pm		
4:00pm		

	ACTION TAKEN	GOAL	RESULT
5:00pm	PROSPECTS	3-10	
6:00pm	CALLS	20-30	
	INTERVIEWS	1-4	
9:00pm	INVITES	2-5	
	MEETINGS	2-3	

	RESULTS CATEGORY	RESULTS
10:00pm	RECRUITS	
11:00pm	SALES	
	RESIDUALS	

PROSPECT GENERATION SHEET

M = Married   C = Children   H = Home Owner   FT = Full-Time Job

NAME	PHONE	NOTES (CIRCLE APPLICABLE)
1		M C H FT
2		M C H FT
3		M C H FT
4		M C H FT
5		M C H FT
6		M C H FT
7		M C H FT
8		M C H FT
9		M C H FT
10		M C H FT

PROSPECT GENERATION SHEET

M = Married   C = Children   H = Home Owner   FT = Full-Time Job

NAME	PHONE	NOTES (CIRCLE APPLICABLE)	
1			M C H FT
2			M C H FT
3			M C H FT
4			M C H FT
5			M C H FT
6			M C H FT
7			M C H FT
8			M C H FT
9			M C H FT
10			M C H FT

FOLLOW UP SHEET

NAME	PHONE	NOTES

DAILY MASSIVE ACTION PLAN

Goals & Affirmations For Day	Time:	Date:

DAILY SCHEDULE	PEOPLE TO CONTACT	THINGS TO DO
6:00am		
7:00am		
8:00am		
9:00am		
10:00am		
11:00am		
12:00 Noon		
1:00pm		
2:00pm		
3:00pm		
4:00pm		

DAILY SCHEDULE	ACTION TAKEN	GOAL	RESULT
5:00pm	PROSPECTS	3-10	
6:00pm	CALLS	20-30	
	INTERVIEWS	1-4	
9:00pm	INVITES	2-5	
	MEETINGS	2-3	

DAILY SCHEDULE	RESULTS CATEGORY	RESULTS	
10:00pm	RECRUITS		
11:00pm	SALES		
	RESIDUALS		

PROSPECT GENERATION SHEET

M = Married   C = Children   H = Home Owner   FT = Full-Time Job

NAME	PHONE	NOTES (CIRCLE APPLICABLE)
1		M C H FT
2		M C H FT
3		M C H FT
4		M C H FT
5		M C H FT
6		M C H FT
7		M C H FT
8		M C H FT
9		M C H FT
10		M C H FT

PROSPECT GENERATION SHEET

M = Married   C = Children   H = Home Owner   FT = Full-Time Job

NAME	PHONE	NOTES (CIRCLE APPLICABLE)
1		M C H FT
2		M C H FT
3		M C H FT
4		M C H FT
5		M C H FT
6		M C H FT
7		M C H FT
8		M C H FT
9		M C H FT
10		M C H FT

FOLLOW UP SHEET

NAME	PHONE	NOTES

DAILY MASSIVE ACTION PLAN

Goals & Affirmations For Day	Time:		Date:	

DAILY SCHEDULE	PEOPLE TO CONTACT	THINGS TO DO
6:00am		
7:00am		
8:00am		
9:00am		
10:00am		
11:00am		
12:00 Noon		
1:00pm		
2:00pm		
3:00pm		
4:00pm		

DAILY SCHEDULE	ACTION TAKEN	GOAL	RESULT
5:00pm	PROSPECTS	3-10	
6:00pm	CALLS	20-30	
	INTERVIEWS	1-4	
9:00pm	INVITES	2-5	
	MEETINGS	2-3	
10:00pm	RESULTS CATEGORY	RESULTS	
	RECRUITS		
11:00pm	SALES		
	RESIDUALS		

PROSPECT GENERATION SHEET

M = Married   C = Children   H = Home Owner   FT = Full-Time Job

NAME	PHONE	NOTES (CIRCLE APPLICABLE)	
1			M C H FT
2			M C H FT
3			M C H FT
4			M C H FT
5			M C H FT
6			M C H FT
7			M C H FT
8			M C H FT
9			M C H FT
10			M C H FT

PROSPECT GENERATION SHEET

M = Married   C = Children   H = Home Owner   FT = Full-Time Job

NAME	PHONE	NOTES (CIRCLE APPLICABLE)	
1			M C H FT
2			M C H FT
3			M C H FT
4			M C H FT
5			M C H FT
6			M C H FT
7			M C H FT
8			M C H FT
9			M C H FT
10			M C H FT

FOLLOW UP SHEET

NAME	PHONE	NOTES

DAILY MASSIVE ACTION PLAN

Goals & Affirmations For Day	Time:	Date:

DAILY SCHEDULE	PEOPLE TO CONTACT	THINGS TO DO
6:00am		
7:00am		
8:00am		
9:00am		
10:00am		
11:00am		
12:00 Noon		
1:00pm		
2:00pm		
3:00pm		
4:00pm		

5:00pm	ACTION TAKEN	GOAL	RESULT
	PROSPECTS	3-10	
6:00pm	CALLS	20-30	
	INTERVIEWS	1-4	
9:00pm	INVITES	2-5	
	MEETINGS	2-3	

10:00pm	RESULTS CATEGORY	RESULTS
	RECRUITS	
11:00pm	SALES	
	RESIDUALS	

PROSPECT GENERATION SHEET

M = Married   C = Children   H = Home Owner   FT = Full-Time Job

NAME	PHONE	NOTES (CIRCLE APPLICABLE)	
1			M C H FT
2			M C H FT
3			M C H FT
4			M C H FT
5			M C H FT
6			M C H FT
7			M C H FT
8			M C H FT
9			M C H FT
10			M C H FT

PROSPECT GENERATION SHEET

M = Married   C = Children   H = Home Owner   FT = Full-Time Job

NAME	PHONE	NOTES (CIRCLE APPLICABLE)	
1			M C H FT
2			M C H FT
3			M C H FT
4			M C H FT
5			M C H FT
6			M C H FT
7			M C H FT
8			M C H FT
9			M C H FT
10			M C H FT

FOLLOW UP SHEET

NAME	PHONE	NOTES

DAILY MASSIVE ACTION PLAN

Goals & Affirmations For Day	Time:	Date:

DAILY SCHEDULE	PEOPLE TO CONTACT	THINGS TO DO
6:00am		
7:00am		
8:00am		
9:00am		
10:00am		
11:00am		
12:00 Noon		
1:00pm		
2:00pm		
3:00pm		
4:00pm		

DAILY SCHEDULE	ACTION TAKEN	GOAL	RESULT
5:00pm	PROSPECTS	3-10	
	CALLS	20-30	
6:00pm	INTERVIEWS	1-4	
	INVITES	2-5	
9:00pm	MEETINGS	2-3	
10:00pm	RESULTS CATEGORY	RESULTS	
	RECRUITS		
11:00pm	SALES		
	RESIDUALS		

PROSPECT GENERATION SHEET

M = Married   C = Children   H = Home Owner   FT = Full-Time Job

NAME	PHONE	NOTES (CIRCLE APPLICABLE)	
1			M C H FT
2			M C H FT
3			M C H FT
4			M C H FT
5			M C H FT
6			M C H FT
7			M C H FT
8			M C H FT
9			M C H FT
10			M C H FT

PROSPECT GENERATION SHEET

M = Married   C = Children   H = Home Owner   FT = Full-Time Job

NAME	PHONE	NOTES (CIRCLE APPLICABLE)	
1			M C H FT
2			M C H FT
3			M C H FT
4			M C H FT
5			M C H FT
6			M C H FT
7			M C H FT
8			M C H FT
9			M C H FT
10			M C H FT

FOLLOW UP SHEET

NAME	PHONE	NOTES

DAILY MASSIVE ACTION PLAN

Goals & Affirmations For Day	Time:		Date:	

DAILY SCHEDULE	PEOPLE TO CONTACT	THINGS TO DO
6:00am		
7:00am		
8:00am		
9:00am		
10:00am		
11:00am		
12:00 Noon		
1:00pm		
2:00pm		
3:00pm		
4:00pm		

	ACTION TAKEN	GOAL	RESULT
5:00pm	PROSPECTS	3-10	
6:00pm	CALLS	20-30	
	INTERVIEWS	1-4	
9:00pm	INVITES	2-5	
	MEETINGS	2-3	

	RESULTS CATEGORY	RESULTS
10:00pm	RECRUITS	
11:00pm	SALES	
	RESIDUALS	

PROSPECT GENERATION SHEET

M = Married   C = Children   H = Home Owner   FT = Full-Time Job

NAME	PHONE	NOTES (CIRCLE APPLICABLE)
1		M C H FT
2		M C H FT
3		M C H FT
4		M C H FT
5		M C H FT
6		M C H FT
7		M C H FT
8		M C H FT
9		M C H FT
10		M C H FT

PROSPECT GENERATION SHEET

M = Married   C = Children   H = Home Owner   FT = Full-Time Job

NAME	PHONE	NOTES (CIRCLE APPLICABLE)
1		M C H FT
2		M C H FT
3		M C H FT
4		M C H FT
5		M C H FT
6		M C H FT
7		M C H FT
8		M C H FT
9		M C H FT
10		M C H FT

FOLLOW UP SHEET

NAME	PHONE	NOTES

MONTH OF: _____

SUNDAY	MONDAY	TUESDAY	WEDNESDAY	THURSDAY	FRIDAY	SATURDAY

Monthly Goals	
Personal Sales	
Team Sales	
Personal Recruits	
Team Recruits	
Monthly Sales Income	
Monthly Residual Income	

Monthly Results	
Personal Sales	
Team Sales	
Personal Recruits	
Team Recruits	
Monthly Sales Income	
Monthly Residual Income	

Month End Review

_____

_____

_____

_____

90-Day Run Notes

WEEKLY ACTIVITY LOG / WEEK OF: _____

Be the Most Productive Person You Can Be At All Times

	SUNDAY	MONDAY	TUESDAY	WEDNESDAY	THURSDAY	FRIDAY	SATURDAY
8am							
9am							
10am							
11am							
12 noon							
1pm							
2pm							
3pm							
4pm							
5pm							
6pm							
7pm							
8pm							
9pm							

Persistence:

"Firm or obstinate continuance in a course of action in spite of difficulty or opposition."

Massive Action Plan To Get $_____ / Yr. Income

Weekly Activity Planner For The Week Of: _____

WEEKLY	GOAL	SUN	MON	TUE	WED	THU	FRI	SAT
PROSPECTS	20							
CALLS	100							
INTERVIEWS	15							
INVITES	10							
MEETINGS	10							
SIGN UPS								
SALES	$							
RESIDUALS	$							

MTD #'s	RECRUITS	RESIDUALS	SALES
PERSONAL			
TEAM			

MEETINGS
1	
2	
3	
4	
5	
6	
7	
8	
9	
10	

PROSPECTS
1	
2	
3	
4	
5	
6	
7	
8	

INTERVIEWS
1	
2	
3	
4	
5	
6	
7	
8	
9	
10	

CALLS
1	
2	
3	
4	
5	
6	
7	
8	
9	
10	
11	
12	
13	
14	
15	

DAILY MASSIVE ACTION PLAN

Goals & Affirmations For Day	Time:	Date:

DAILY SCHEDULE	PEOPLE TO CONTACT	THINGS TO DO
6:00am		
7:00am		
8:00am		
9:00am		
10:00am		
11:00am		
12:00 Noon		
1:00pm		
2:00pm		
3:00pm		
4:00pm		

	ACTION TAKEN	GOAL	RESULT
5:00pm	PROSPECTS	3-10	
6:00pm	CALLS	20-30	
	INTERVIEWS	1-4	
9:00pm	INVITES	2-5	
	MEETINGS	2-3	

	RESULTS CATEGORY	RESULTS
10:00pm	RECRUITS	
11:00pm	SALES	
	RESIDUALS	

PROSPECT GENERATION SHEET

M = Married   C = Children   H = Home Owner   FT = Full-Time Job

NAME	PHONE	NOTES (CIRCLE APPLICABLE)	
1			M C H FT
2			M C H FT
3			M C H FT
4			M C H FT
5			M C H FT
6			M C H FT
7			M C H FT
8			M C H FT
9			M C H FT
10			M C H FT

PROSPECT GENERATION SHEET

M = Married   C = Children   H = Home Owner   FT = Full-Time Job

NAME	PHONE	NOTES (CIRCLE APPLICABLE)	
1			M C H FT
2			M C H FT
3			M C H FT
4			M C H FT
5			M C H FT
6			M C H FT
7			M C H FT
8			M C H FT
9			M C H FT
10			M C H FT

FOLLOW UP SHEET

NAME	PHONE	NOTES

DAILY MASSIVE ACTION PLAN

Goals & Affirmations For Day	Time:	Date:

DAILY SCHEDULE	PEOPLE TO CONTACT	THINGS TO DO
6:00am		
7:00am		
8:00am		
9:00am		
10:00am		
11:00am		
12:00 Noon		
1:00pm		
2:00pm		
3:00pm		
4:00pm		

DAILY SCHEDULE	ACTION TAKEN	GOAL	RESULT
5:00pm	PROSPECTS	3-10	
6:00pm	CALLS	20-30	
	INTERVIEWS	1-4	
9:00pm	INVITES	2-5	
	MEETINGS	2-3	
10:00pm	RESULTS CATEGORY	RESULTS	
	RECRUITS		
11:00pm	SALES		
	RESIDUALS		

PROSPECT GENERATION SHEET

M = Married   C = Children   H = Home Owner   FT = Full-Time Job

NAME	PHONE	NOTES (CIRCLE APPLICABLE)
1		M C H FT
2		M C H FT
3		M C H FT
4		M C H FT
5		M C H FT
6		M C H FT
7		M C H FT
8		M C H FT
9		M C H FT
10		M C H FT

PROSPECT GENERATION SHEET

M = Married   C = Children   H = Home Owner   FT = Full-Time Job

NAME	PHONE	NOTES (CIRCLE APPLICABLE)
1		M C H FT
2		M C H FT
3		M C H FT
4		M C H FT
5		M C H FT
6		M C H FT
7		M C H FT
8		M C H FT
9		M C H FT
10		M C H FT

FOLLOW UP SHEET

NAME	PHONE	NOTES

DAILY MASSIVE ACTION PLAN

Goals & Affirmations For Day	Time:	Date:

DAILY SCHEDULE	PEOPLE TO CONTACT	THINGS TO DO
6:00am		
7:00am		
8:00am		
9:00am		
10:00am		
11:00am		
12:00 Noon		
1:00pm		
2:00pm		
3:00pm		
4:00pm		

DAILY SCHEDULE	ACTION TAKEN	GOAL	RESULT
5:00pm	PROSPECTS	3-10	
6:00pm	CALLS	20-30	
	INTERVIEWS	1-4	
9:00pm	INVITES	2-5	
	MEETINGS	2-3	

DAILY SCHEDULE	RESULTS CATEGORY	RESULTS	
10:00pm	RECRUITS		
11:00pm	SALES		
	RESIDUALS		

PROSPECT GENERATION SHEET

M = Married   C = Children   H = Home Owner   FT = Full-Time Job

NAME	PHONE	NOTES (CIRCLE APPLICABLE)	
1			M C H FT
2			M C H FT
3			M C H FT
4			M C H FT
5			M C H FT
6			M C H FT
7			M C H FT
8			M C H FT
9			M C H FT
10			M C H FT

PROSPECT GENERATION SHEET

M = Married   C = Children   H = Home Owner   FT = Full-Time Job

	NAME	PHONE	NOTES (CIRCLE APPLICABLE)
1			M C H FT
2			M C H FT
3			M C H FT
4			M C H FT
5			M C H FT
6			M C H FT
7			M C H FT
8			M C H FT
9			M C H FT
10			M C H FT

FOLLOW UP SHEET

NAME	PHONE	NOTES

DAILY MASSIVE ACTION PLAN

Goals & Affirmations For Day	Time:	Date:

DAILY SCHEDULE	PEOPLE TO CONTACT	THINGS TO DO
6:00am		
7:00am		
8:00am		
9:00am		
10:00am		
11:00am		
12:00 Noon		
1:00pm		
2:00pm		
3:00pm		
4:00pm		

DAILY SCHEDULE	ACTION TAKEN	GOAL	RESULT
5:00pm	PROSPECTS	3-10	
6:00pm	CALLS	20-30	
	INTERVIEWS	1-4	
9:00pm	INVITES	2-5	
	MEETINGS	2-3	

DAILY SCHEDULE	RESULTS CATEGORY	RESULTS	
10:00pm	RECRUITS		
11:00pm	SALES		
	RESIDUALS		

PROSPECT GENERATION SHEET

M = Married   C = Children   H = Home Owner   FT = Full-Time Job

NAME	PHONE	NOTES (CIRCLE APPLICABLE)
1		M C H FT
2		M C H FT
3		M C H FT
4		M C H FT
5		M C H FT
6		M C H FT
7		M C H FT
8		M C H FT
9		M C H FT
10		M C H FT

PROSPECT GENERATION SHEET

M = Married   C = Children   H = Home Owner   FT = Full-Time Job

NAME	PHONE	NOTES (CIRCLE APPLICABLE)
1		M C H FT
2		M C H FT
3		M C H FT
4		M C H FT
5		M C H FT
6		M C H FT
7		M C H FT
8		M C H FT
9		M C H FT
10		M C H FT

FOLLOW UP SHEET

NAME	PHONE	NOTES

DAILY MASSIVE ACTION PLAN

Goals & Affirmations For Day	Time:	Date:

DAILY SCHEDULE	PEOPLE TO CONTACT	THINGS TO DO
6:00am		
7:00am		
8:00am		
9:00am		
10:00am		
11:00am		
12:00 Noon		
1:00pm		
2:00pm		
3:00pm		
4:00pm		

	ACTION TAKEN	GOAL	RESULT
5:00pm	PROSPECTS	3-10	
6:00pm	CALLS	20-30	
	INTERVIEWS	1-4	
9:00pm	INVITES	2-5	
	MEETINGS	2-3	
10:00pm	RESULTS CATEGORY	RESULTS	
	RECRUITS		
11:00pm	SALES		
	RESIDUALS		

PROSPECT GENERATION SHEET

M = Married   C = Children   H = Home Owner   FT = Full-Time Job

NAME	PHONE	NOTES (CIRCLE APPLICABLE)
1		M C H FT
2		M C H FT
3		M C H FT
4		M C H FT
5		M C H FT
6		M C H FT
7		M C H FT
8		M C H FT
9		M C H FT
10		M C H FT

PROSPECT GENERATION SHEET

M = Married   C = Children   H = Home Owner   FT = Full-Time Job

NAME	PHONE	NOTES (CIRCLE APPLICABLE)
1		M C H FT
2		M C H FT
3		M C H FT
4		M C H FT
5		M C H FT
6		M C H FT
7		M C H FT
8		M C H FT
9		M C H FT
10		M C H FT

FOLLOW UP SHEET

NAME	PHONE	NOTES

DAILY MASSIVE ACTION PLAN

Goals & Affirmations For Day		Time:		Date:	

DAILY SCHEDULE	PEOPLE TO CONTACT	THINGS TO DO
6:00am		
7:00am		
8:00am		
9:00am		
10:00am		
11:00am		
12:00 Noon		
1:00pm		
2:00pm		
3:00pm		
4:00pm		

DAILY SCHEDULE	ACTION TAKEN	GOAL	RESULT
5:00pm	PROSPECTS	3-10	
6:00pm	CALLS	20-30	
	INTERVIEWS	1-4	
9:00pm	INVITES	2-5	
	MEETINGS	2-3	

DAILY SCHEDULE	RESULTS CATEGORY	RESULTS	
10:00pm	RECRUITS		
11:00pm	SALES		
	RESIDUALS		

PROSPECT GENERATION SHEET

M = Married   C = Children   H = Home Owner   FT = Full-Time Job

NAME	PHONE	NOTES (CIRCLE APPLICABLE)	
1			M C H FT
2			M C H FT
3			M C H FT
4			M C H FT
5			M C H FT
6			M C H FT
7			M C H FT
8			M C H FT
9			M C H FT
10			M C H FT

PROSPECT GENERATION SHEET

M = Married   C = Children   H = Home Owner   FT = Full-Time Job

NAME	PHONE	NOTES (CIRCLE APPLICABLE)
1		M C H FT
2		M C H FT
3		M C H FT
4		M C H FT
5		M C H FT
6		M C H FT
7		M C H FT
8		M C H FT
9		M C H FT
10		M C H FT

FOLLOW UP SHEET

NAME	PHONE	NOTES

DAILY MASSIVE ACTION PLAN

Goals & Affirmations For Day	Time:	Date:

DAILY SCHEDULE	PEOPLE TO CONTACT	THINGS TO DO
6:00am		
7:00am		
8:00am		
9:00am		
10:00am		
11:00am		
12:00 Noon		
1:00pm		
2:00pm		
3:00pm		
4:00pm		

DAILY SCHEDULE	ACTION TAKEN	GOAL	RESULT
5:00pm	PROSPECTS	3-10	
6:00pm	CALLS	20-30	
	INTERVIEWS	1-4	
9:00pm	INVITES	2-5	
	MEETINGS	2-3	
10:00pm	RESULTS CATEGORY	RESULTS	
	RECRUITS		
11:00pm	SALES		
	RESIDUALS		

PROSPECT GENERATION SHEET

M = Married   C = Children   H = Home Owner   FT = Full-Time Job

NAME	PHONE	NOTES (CIRCLE APPLICABLE)	
1			M C H FT
2			M C H FT
3			M C H FT
4			M C H FT
5			M C H FT
6			M C H FT
7			M C H FT
8			M C H FT
9			M C H FT
10			M C H FT

PROSPECT GENERATION SHEET

M = Married   C = Children   H = Home Owner   FT = Full-Time Job

NAME	PHONE	NOTES (CIRCLE APPLICABLE)
1		M C H FT
2		M C H FT
3		M C H FT
4		M C H FT
5		M C H FT
6		M C H FT
7		M C H FT
8		M C H FT
9		M C H FT
10		M C H FT

FOLLOW UP SHEET

NAME	PHONE	NOTES

WEEKLY ACTIVITY LOG / WEEK OF: _____

Be the Most Productive Person You Can Be At All Times

	SUNDAY	MONDAY	TUESDAY	WEDNESDAY	THURSDAY	FRIDAY	SATURDAY
8am							
9am							
10am							
11am							
12 noon							
1pm							
2pm							
3pm							
4pm							
5pm							
6pm							
7pm							
8pm							
9pm							

Persistence:

"Firm or obstinate continuance in a course of action in spite of difficulty or opposition."

Massive Action Plan To Get $_____ / Yr. Income

Weekly Activity Planner For The Week Of: _____

WEEKLY	GOAL	SUN	MON	TUE	WED	THU	FRI	SAT
PROSPECTS	20							
CALLS	100							
INTERVIEWS	15							
INVITES	10							
MEETINGS	10							
SIGN UPS								
SALES	$							
RESIDUALS	$							

MTD #'s	RECRUITS	RESIDUALS	SALES
PERSONAL			
TEAM			

PROSPECTS

1
2
3
4
5
6
7
8

MEETINGS

1
2
3
4
5
6
7
8
9
10

INTERVIEWS

1
2
3
4
5
6
7
8
9
10

CALLS

1
2
3
4
5
6
7
8
9
10
11
12
13
14
15

DAILY MASSIVE ACTION PLAN

Goals & Affirmations For Day	Time:	Date:

DAILY SCHEDULE	PEOPLE TO CONTACT	THINGS TO DO
6:00am		
7:00am		
8:00am		
9:00am		
10:00am		
11:00am		
12:00 Noon		
1:00pm		
2:00pm		
3:00pm		
4:00pm		

DAILY SCHEDULE	ACTION TAKEN	GOAL	RESULT
5:00pm	PROSPECTS	3-10	
6:00pm	CALLS	20-30	
	INTERVIEWS	1-4	
9:00pm	INVITES	2-5	
	MEETINGS	2-3	
10:00pm	RESULTS CATEGORY	RESULTS	
	RECRUITS		
11:00pm	SALES		
	RESIDUALS		

PROSPECT GENERATION SHEET

M = Married   C = Children   H = Home Owner   FT = Full-Time Job

NAME	PHONE	NOTES (CIRCLE APPLICABLE)	
1			M C H FT
2			M C H FT
3			M C H FT
4			M C H FT
5			M C H FT
6			M C H FT
7			M C H FT
8			M C H FT
9			M C H FT
10			M C H FT

PROSPECT GENERATION SHEET

M = Married   C = Children   H = Home Owner   FT = Full-Time Job

NAME	PHONE	NOTES (CIRCLE APPLICABLE)	
1			M C H FT
2			M C H FT
3			M C H FT
4			M C H FT
5			M C H FT
6			M C H FT
7			M C H FT
8			M C H FT
9			M C H FT
10			M C H FT

FOLLOW UP SHEET

NAME	PHONE	NOTES

DAILY MASSIVE ACTION PLAN

Goals & Affirmations For Day	Time:	Date:

DAILY SCHEDULE	PEOPLE TO CONTACT	THINGS TO DO
6:00am		
7:00am		
8:00am		
9:00am		
10:00am		
11:00am		
12:00 Noon		
1:00pm		
2:00pm		
3:00pm		
4:00pm		

DAILY SCHEDULE	ACTION TAKEN	GOAL	RESULT
5:00pm	PROSPECTS	3-10	
6:00pm	CALLS	20-30	
	INTERVIEWS	1-4	
9:00pm	INVITES	2-5	
	MEETINGS	2-3	
10:00pm	**RESULTS CATEGORY**	**RESULTS**	
	RECRUITS		
11:00pm	SALES		
	RESIDUALS		

PROSPECT GENERATION SHEET

M = Married   C = Children   H = Home Owner   FT = Full-Time Job

NAME	PHONE	NOTES (CIRCLE APPLICABLE)
1		M C H FT
2		M C H FT
3		M C H FT
4		M C H FT
5		M C H FT
6		M C H FT
7		M C H FT
8		M C H FT
9		M C H FT
10		M C H FT

PROSPECT GENERATION SHEET

M = Married   C = Children   H = Home Owner   FT = Full-Time Job

NAME	PHONE	NOTES (CIRCLE APPLICABLE)	
1			M C H FT
2			M C H FT
3			M C H FT
4			M C H FT
5			M C H FT
6			M C H FT
7			M C H FT
8			M C H FT
9			M C H FT
10			M C H FT

FOLLOW UP SHEET

NAME	PHONE	NOTES

DAILY MASSIVE ACTION PLAN

Goals & Affirmations For Day	Time:	Date:

DAILY SCHEDULE	PEOPLE TO CONTACT	THINGS TO DO
6:00am		
7:00am		
8:00am		
9:00am		
10:00am		
11:00am		
12:00 Noon		
1:00pm		
2:00pm		
3:00pm		
4:00pm		

DAILY SCHEDULE	ACTION TAKEN	GOAL	RESULT
5:00pm	PROSPECTS	3-10	
6:00pm	CALLS	20-30	
	INTERVIEWS	1-4	
9:00pm	INVITES	2-5	
	MEETINGS	2-3	
10:00pm	RESULTS CATEGORY	RESULTS	
	RECRUITS		
11:00pm	SALES		
	RESIDUALS		

PROSPECT GENERATION SHEET

M = Married   C = Children   H = Home Owner   FT = Full-Time Job

NAME	PHONE	NOTES (CIRCLE APPLICABLE)	
1			M C H FT
2			M C H FT
3			M C H FT
4			M C H FT
5			M C H FT
6			M C H FT
7			M C H FT
8			M C H FT
9			M C H FT
10			M C H FT

PROSPECT GENERATION SHEET

M = Married   C = Children   H = Home Owner   FT = Full-Time Job

NAME	PHONE	NOTES (CIRCLE APPLICABLE)	
1			M C H FT
2			M C H FT
3			M C H FT
4			M C H FT
5			M C H FT
6			M C H FT
7			M C H FT
8			M C H FT
9			M C H FT
10			M C H FT

FOLLOW UP SHEET

NAME	PHONE	NOTES

DAILY MASSIVE ACTION PLAN

Goals & Affirmations For Day		Time:		Date:	

DAILY SCHEDULE	PEOPLE TO CONTACT	THINGS TO DO
6:00am		
7:00am		
8:00am		
9:00am		
10:00am		
11:00am		
12:00 Noon		
1:00pm		
2:00pm		
3:00pm		
4:00pm		

DAILY SCHEDULE	ACTION TAKEN	GOAL	RESULT
5:00pm	PROSPECTS	3-10	
	CALLS	20-30	
6:00pm	INTERVIEWS	1-4	
	INVITES	2-5	
9:00pm	MEETINGS	2-3	
10:00pm	RESULTS CATEGORY	RESULTS	
	RECRUITS		
11:00pm	SALES		
	RESIDUALS		

PROSPECT GENERATION SHEET

M = Married   C = Children   H = Home Owner   FT = Full-Time Job

NAME	PHONE	NOTES (CIRCLE APPLICABLE)
1		M C H FT
2		M C H FT
3		M C H FT
4		M C H FT
5		M C H FT
6		M C H FT
7		M C H FT
8		M C H FT
9		M C H FT
10		M C H FT

PROSPECT GENERATION SHEET

M = Married   C = Children   H = Home Owner   FT = Full-Time Job

NAME	PHONE	NOTES (CIRCLE APPLICABLE)	
1			M C H FT
2			M C H FT
3			M C H FT
4			M C H FT
5			M C H FT
6			M C H FT
7			M C H FT
8			M C H FT
9			M C H FT
10			M C H FT

FOLLOW UP SHEET

NAME	PHONE	NOTES

DAILY MASSIVE ACTION PLAN

Goals & Affirmations For Day	Time:	Date:

DAILY SCHEDULE	PEOPLE TO CONTACT	THINGS TO DO
6:00am		
7:00am		
8:00am		
9:00am		
10:00am		
11:00am		
12:00 Noon		
1:00pm		
2:00pm		
3:00pm		
4:00pm		

DAILY SCHEDULE	ACTION TAKEN	GOAL	RESULT
5:00pm	PROSPECTS	3-10	
6:00pm	CALLS	20-30	
	INTERVIEWS	1-4	
9:00pm	INVITES	2-5	
	MEETINGS	2-3	
10:00pm	RESULTS CATEGORY	RESULTS	
	RECRUITS		
11:00pm	SALES		
	RESIDUALS		

PROSPECT GENERATION SHEET

M = Married   C = Children   H = Home Owner   FT = Full-Time Job

NAME	PHONE	NOTES (CIRCLE APPLICABLE)	
1			M C H FT
2			M C H FT
3			M C H FT
4			M C H FT
5			M C H FT
6			M C H FT
7			M C H FT
8			M C H FT
9			M C H FT
10			M C H FT

PROSPECT GENERATION SHEET

M = Married   C = Children   H = Home Owner   FT = Full-Time Job

NAME	PHONE	NOTES (CIRCLE APPLICABLE)	
1			M C H FT
2			M C H FT
3			M C H FT
4			M C H FT
5			M C H FT
6			M C H FT
7			M C H FT
8			M C H FT
9			M C H FT
10			M C H FT

FOLLOW UP SHEET

NAME	PHONE	NOTES

DAILY MASSIVE ACTION PLAN

Goals & Affirmations For Day	Time:	Date:

DAILY SCHEDULE	PEOPLE TO CONTACT	THINGS TO DO
6:00am		
7:00am		
8:00am		
9:00am		
10:00am		
11:00am		
12:00 Noon		
1:00pm		
2:00pm		
3:00pm		
4:00pm		

DAILY SCHEDULE	ACTION TAKEN	GOAL	RESULT
5:00pm	PROSPECTS	3-10	
	CALLS	20-30	
6:00pm	INTERVIEWS	1-4	
	INVITES	2-5	
9:00pm	MEETINGS	2-3	
	RESULTS CATEGORY	RESULTS	
10:00pm	RECRUITS		
	SALES		
11:00pm	RESIDUALS		

PROSPECT GENERATION SHEET

M = Married   C = Children   H = Home Owner   FT = Full-Time Job

NAME	PHONE	NOTES (CIRCLE APPLICABLE)
1		M C H FT
2		M C H FT
3		M C H FT
4		M C H FT
5		M C H FT
6		M C H FT
7		M C H FT
8		M C H FT
9		M C H FT
10		M C H FT

PROSPECT GENERATION SHEET

M = Married   C = Children   H = Home Owner   FT = Full-Time Job

	NAME	PHONE	NOTES (CIRCLE APPLICABLE)
1			M C H FT
2			M C H FT
3			M C H FT
4			M C H FT
5			M C H FT
6			M C H FT
7			M C H FT
8			M C H FT
9			M C H FT
10			M C H FT

FOLLOW UP SHEET

NAME	PHONE	NOTES

DAILY MASSIVE ACTION PLAN

Goals & Affirmations For Day	Time:		Date:	

DAILY SCHEDULE	PEOPLE TO CONTACT	THINGS TO DO
6:00am		
7:00am		
8:00am		
9:00am		
10:00am		
11:00am		
12:00 Noon		
1:00pm		
2:00pm		
3:00pm		
4:00pm		

DAILY SCHEDULE (cont)	ACTION TAKEN	GOAL	RESULT
5:00pm	PROSPECTS	3-10	
6:00pm	CALLS	20-30	
	INTERVIEWS	1-4	
9:00pm	INVITES	2-5	
	MEETINGS	2-3	

	RESULTS CATEGORY	RESULTS	
10:00pm	RECRUITS		
11:00pm	SALES		
	RESIDUALS		

PROSPECT GENERATION SHEET

M = Married   C = Children   H = Home Owner   FT = Full-Time Job

NAME	PHONE	NOTES (CIRCLE APPLICABLE)
1		M C H FT
2		M C H FT
3		M C H FT
4		M C H FT
5		M C H FT
6		M C H FT
7		M C H FT
8		M C H FT
9		M C H FT
10		M C H FT

PROSPECT GENERATION SHEET

M = Married   C = Children   H = Home Owner   FT = Full-Time Job

NAME	PHONE	NOTES (CIRCLE APPLICABLE)	
1			M C H FT
2			M C H FT
3			M C H FT
4			M C H FT
5			M C H FT
6			M C H FT
7			M C H FT
8			M C H FT
9			M C H FT
10			M C H FT

FOLLOW UP SHEET

NAME	PHONE	NOTES

WEEKLY ACTIVITY LOG / WEEK OF: _____

Be the Most Productive Person You Can Be At All Times

	SUNDAY	MONDAY	TUESDAY	WEDNESDAY	THURSDAY	FRIDAY	SATURDAY
8am							
9am							
10am							
11am							
12 noon							
1pm							
2pm							
3pm							
4pm							
5pm							
6pm							
7pm							
8pm							
9pm							

Persistence:

"Firm or obstinate continuance in a course of action in spite of difficulty or opposition."

Massive Action Plan To Get $_____ / Yr. Income

Weekly Activity Planner For The Week Of: _____

WEEKLY	GOAL	SUN	MON	TUE	WED	THU	FRI	SAT
PROSPECTS	20							
CALLS	100							
INTERVIEWS	15							
INVITES	10							
MEETINGS	10							
SIGN UPS								
SALES	$							
RESIDUALS	$							

MTD #'s	RECRUITS	RESIDUALS	SALES
PERSONAL			
TEAM			

PROSPECTS
1.
2.
3.
4.
5.
6.
7.
8.

MEETINGS
1.
2.
3.
4.
5.
6.
7.
8.
9.
10.

INTERVIEWS
1.
2.
3.
4.
5.
6.
7.
8.
9.
10.

CALLS
1.
2.
3.
4.
5.
6.
7.
8.
9.
10.
11.
12.
13.
14.
15.

DAILY MASSIVE ACTION PLAN

Goals & Affirmations For Day	Time:	Date:

DAILY SCHEDULE	PEOPLE TO CONTACT	THINGS TO DO
6:00am		
7:00am		
8:00am		
9:00am		
10:00am		
11:00am		
12:00 Noon		
1:00pm		
2:00pm		
3:00pm		
4:00pm		

DAILY SCHEDULE	ACTION TAKEN	GOAL	RESULT
5:00pm	PROSPECTS	3-10	
6:00pm	CALLS	20-30	
	INTERVIEWS	1-4	
9:00pm	INVITES	2-5	
	MEETINGS	2-3	

	RESULTS CATEGORY	RESULTS	
10:00pm	RECRUITS		
11:00pm	SALES		
	RESIDUALS		

PROSPECT GENERATION SHEET

M = Married   C = Children   H = Home Owner   FT = Full-Time Job

NAME	PHONE	NOTES (CIRCLE APPLICABLE)
1		M C H FT
2		M C H FT
3		M C H FT
4		M C H FT
5		M C H FT
6		M C H FT
7		M C H FT
8		M C H FT
9		M C H FT
10		M C H FT

PROSPECT GENERATION SHEET

M = Married   C = Children   H = Home Owner   FT = Full-Time Job

NAME	PHONE	NOTES (CIRCLE APPLICABLE)
1		M C H FT
2		M C H FT
3		M C H FT
4		M C H FT
5		M C H FT
6		M C H FT
7		M C H FT
8		M C H FT
9		M C H FT
10		M C H FT

FOLLOW UP SHEET

NAME	PHONE	NOTES

DAILY MASSIVE ACTION PLAN

Goals & Affirmations For Day	Time:	Date:

DAILY SCHEDULE	PEOPLE TO CONTACT	THINGS TO DO
6:00am		
7:00am		
8:00am		
9:00am		
10:00am		
11:00am		
12:00 Noon		
1:00pm		
2:00pm		
3:00pm		
4:00pm		

DAILY SCHEDULE	ACTION TAKEN	GOAL	RESULT
5:00pm	PROSPECTS	3-10	
6:00pm	CALLS	20-30	
	INTERVIEWS	1-4	
9:00pm	INVITES	2-5	
	MEETINGS	2-3	
10:00pm	RESULTS CATEGORY	RESULTS	
	RECRUITS		
11:00pm	SALES		
	RESIDUALS		

PROSPECT GENERATION SHEET

M = Married   C = Children   H = Home Owner   FT = Full-Time Job

NAME	PHONE	NOTES (CIRCLE APPLICABLE)
1		M C H FT
2		M C H FT
3		M C H FT
4		M C H FT
5		M C H FT
6		M C H FT
7		M C H FT
8		M C H FT
9		M C H FT
10		M C H FT

PROSPECT GENERATION SHEET

M = Married   C = Children   H = Home Owner   FT = Full-Time Job

NAME	PHONE	NOTES (CIRCLE APPLICABLE)
1		M C H FT
2		M C H FT
3		M C H FT
4		M C H FT
5		M C H FT
6		M C H FT
7		M C H FT
8		M C H FT
9		M C H FT
10		M C H FT

FOLLOW UP SHEET

NAME	PHONE	NOTES

DAILY MASSIVE ACTION PLAN

Goals & Affirmations For Day	Time:	Date:

DAILY SCHEDULE	PEOPLE TO CONTACT	THINGS TO DO
6:00am		
7:00am		
8:00am		
9:00am		
10:00am		
11:00am		
12:00 Noon		
1:00pm		
2:00pm		
3:00pm		
4:00pm		

	ACTION TAKEN	GOAL	RESULT
5:00pm	PROSPECTS	3-10	
6:00pm	CALLS	20-30	
	INTERVIEWS	1-4	
9:00pm	INVITES	2-5	
	MEETINGS	2-3	

	RESULTS CATEGORY	RESULTS
10:00pm	RECRUITS	
11:00pm	SALES	
	RESIDUALS	

PROSPECT GENERATION SHEET

M = Married   C = Children   H = Home Owner   FT = Full-Time Job

NAME	PHONE	NOTES (CIRCLE APPLICABLE)	
1			M C H FT
2			M C H FT
3			M C H FT
4			M C H FT
5			M C H FT
6			M C H FT
7			M C H FT
8			M C H FT
9			M C H FT
10			M C H FT

PROSPECT GENERATION SHEET

M = Married   C = Children   H = Home Owner   FT = Full-Time Job

NAME	PHONE	NOTES (CIRCLE APPLICABLE)
1		M C H FT
2		M C H FT
3		M C H FT
4		M C H FT
5		M C H FT
6		M C H FT
7		M C H FT
8		M C H FT
9		M C H FT
10		M C H FT

FOLLOW UP SHEET

NAME	PHONE	NOTES

DAILY MASSIVE ACTION PLAN

Goals & Affirmations For Day	Time:		Date:	

DAILY SCHEDULE	PEOPLE TO CONTACT	THINGS TO DO
6:00am		
7:00am		
8:00am		
9:00am		
10:00am		
11:00am		
12:00 Noon		
1:00pm		
2:00pm		
3:00pm		
4:00pm		

DAILY SCHEDULE	ACTION TAKEN	GOAL	RESULT
5:00pm	PROSPECTS	3-10	
6:00pm	CALLS	20-30	
	INTERVIEWS	1-4	
9:00pm	INVITES	2-5	
	MEETINGS	2-3	
10:00pm	RESULTS CATEGORY	RESULTS	
	RECRUITS		
11:00pm	SALES		
	RESIDUALS		

PROSPECT GENERATION SHEET

M = Married   C = Children   H = Home Owner   FT = Full-Time Job

NAME	PHONE	NOTES (CIRCLE APPLICABLE)	
1			M C H FT
2			M C H FT
3			M C H FT
4			M C H FT
5			M C H FT
6			M C H FT
7			M C H FT
8			M C H FT
9			M C H FT
10			M C H FT

PROSPECT GENERATION SHEET

M = Married   C = Children   H = Home Owner   FT = Full-Time Job

NAME	PHONE	NOTES (CIRCLE APPLICABLE)	
1			M C H FT
2			M C H FT
3			M C H FT
4			M C H FT
5			M C H FT
6			M C H FT
7			M C H FT
8			M C H FT
9			M C H FT
10			M C H FT

FOLLOW UP SHEET

NAME	PHONE	NOTES

DAILY MASSIVE ACTION PLAN

Goals & Affirmations For Day	Time:	Date:

DAILY SCHEDULE	PEOPLE TO CONTACT	THINGS TO DO
6:00am		
7:00am		
8:00am		
9:00am		
10:00am		
11:00am		
12:00 Noon		
1:00pm		
2:00pm		
3:00pm		
4:00pm		

DAILY SCHEDULE	ACTION TAKEN	GOAL	RESULT
5:00pm	PROSPECTS	3-10	
6:00pm	CALLS	20-30	
	INTERVIEWS	1-4	
9:00pm	INVITES	2-5	
	MEETINGS	2-3	

	RESULTS CATEGORY	RESULTS
10:00pm	RECRUITS	
11:00pm	SALES	
	RESIDUALS	

PROSPECT GENERATION SHEET

M = Married   C = Children   H = Home Owner   FT = Full-Time Job

	NAME	PHONE	NOTES (CIRCLE APPLICABLE)
1			M C H FT
2			M C H FT
3			M C H FT
4			M C H FT
5			M C H FT
6			M C H FT
7			M C H FT
8			M C H FT
9			M C H FT
10			M C H FT

PROSPECT GENERATION SHEET

M = Married   C = Children   H = Home Owner   FT = Full-Time Job

NAME	PHONE	NOTES (CIRCLE APPLICABLE)
1		M C H FT
2		M C H FT
3		M C H FT
4		M C H FT
5		M C H FT
6		M C H FT
7		M C H FT
8		M C H FT
9		M C H FT
10		M C H FT

FOLLOW UP SHEET

NAME	PHONE	NOTES

DAILY MASSIVE ACTION PLAN

Goals & Affirmations For Day	Time:	Date:

DAILY SCHEDULE	PEOPLE TO CONTACT	THINGS TO DO
6:00am		
7:00am		
8:00am		
9:00am		
10:00am		
11:00am		
12:00 Noon		
1:00pm		
2:00pm		
3:00pm		
4:00pm		

DAILY SCHEDULE	ACTION TAKEN	GOAL	RESULT
5:00pm	PROSPECTS	3-10	
	CALLS	20-30	
6:00pm	INTERVIEWS	1-4	
	INVITES	2-5	
9:00pm	MEETINGS	2-3	
	RESULTS CATEGORY	RESULTS	
10:00pm	RECRUITS		
	SALES		
11:00pm	RESIDUALS		

PROSPECT GENERATION SHEET

M = Married   C = Children   H = Home Owner   FT = Full-Time Job

NAME	PHONE	NOTES (CIRCLE APPLICABLE)
1		M C H FT
2		M C H FT
3		M C H FT
4		M C H FT
5		M C H FT
6		M C H FT
7		M C H FT
8		M C H FT
9		M C H FT
10		M C H FT

PROSPECT GENERATION SHEET

M = Married   C = Children   H = Home Owner   FT = Full-Time Job

NAME	PHONE	NOTES (CIRCLE APPLICABLE)	
1			M C H FT
2			M C H FT
3			M C H FT
4			M C H FT
5			M C H FT
6			M C H FT
7			M C H FT
8			M C H FT
9			M C H FT
10			M C H FT

FOLLOW UP SHEET

NAME	PHONE	NOTES

DAILY MASSIVE ACTION PLAN

Goals & Affirmations For Day	Time:	Date:

DAILY SCHEDULE	PEOPLE TO CONTACT	THINGS TO DO
6:00am		
7:00am		
8:00am		
9:00am		
10:00am		
11:00am		
12:00 Noon		
1:00pm		
2:00pm		
3:00pm		
4:00pm		

	ACTION TAKEN	GOAL	RESULT
5:00pm	PROSPECTS	3-10	
6:00pm	CALLS	20-30	
	INTERVIEWS	1-4	
9:00pm	INVITES	2-5	
	MEETINGS	2-3	

	RESULTS CATEGORY	RESULTS	
10:00pm	RECRUITS		
11:00pm	SALES		
	RESIDUALS		

PROSPECT GENERATION SHEET

M = Married   C = Children   H = Home Owner   FT = Full-Time Job

NAME	PHONE	NOTES (CIRCLE APPLICABLE)
1		M C H FT
2		M C H FT
3		M C H FT
4		M C H FT
5		M C H FT
6		M C H FT
7		M C H FT
8		M C H FT
9		M C H FT
10		M C H FT

PROSPECT GENERATION SHEET

M = Married C = Children H = Home Owner FT = Full-Time Job

NAME	PHONE	NOTES (CIRCLE APPLICABLE)
1		M C H FT
2		M C H FT
3		M C H FT
4		M C H FT
5		M C H FT
6		M C H FT
7		M C H FT
8		M C H FT
9		M C H FT
10		M C H FT

FOLLOW UP SHEET

NAME	PHONE	NOTES

WEEKLY ACTIVITY LOG / WEEK OF: _____

Be the Most Productive Person You Can Be At All Times

	SUNDAY	MONDAY	TUESDAY	WEDNESDAY	THURSDAY	FRIDAY	SATURDAY
8am							
9am							
10am							
11am							
12 noon							
1pm							
2pm							
3pm							
4pm							
5pm							
6pm							
7pm							
8pm							
9pm							

Persistence:

"Firm or obstinate continuance in a course of action in spite of difficulty or opposition."

Massive Action Plan To Get $_____ / Yr. Income

Weekly Activity Planner For The Week Of: _____

WEEKLY	GOAL	SUN	MON	TUE	WED	THU	FRI	SAT
PROSPECTS	20							
CALLS	100							
INTERVIEWS	15							
INVITES	10							
MEETINGS	10							
SIGN UPS								
SALES	$							
RESIDUALS	$							

MTD #'s	RECRUITS	RESIDUALS	SALES
PERSONAL			
TEAM			

MEETINGS
1
2
3
4
5
6
7
8
9
10

INTERVIEWS
1
2
3
4
5
6
7
8
9
10

PROSPECTS
1
2
3
4
5
6
7
8

CALLS
1
2
3
4
5
6
7
8
9
10
11
12
13
14
15

DAILY MASSIVE ACTION PLAN

Goals & Affirmations For Day	Time:	Date:

DAILY SCHEDULE	PEOPLE TO CONTACT	THINGS TO DO
6:00am		
7:00am		
8:00am		
9:00am		
10:00am		
11:00am		
12:00 Noon		
1:00pm		
2:00pm		
3:00pm		
4:00pm		

DAILY SCHEDULE	ACTION TAKEN	GOAL	RESULT
5:00pm	PROSPECTS	3-10	
6:00pm	CALLS	20-30	
	INTERVIEWS	1-4	
9:00pm	INVITES	2-5	
	MEETINGS	2-3	
10:00pm	RESULTS CATEGORY	RESULTS	
	RECRUITS		
11:00pm	SALES		
	RESIDUALS		

PROSPECT GENERATION SHEET

M = Married   C = Children   H = Home Owner   FT = Full-Time Job

NAME	PHONE	NOTES (CIRCLE APPLICABLE)	
1			M C H FT
2			M C H FT
3			M C H FT
4			M C H FT
5			M C H FT
6			M C H FT
7			M C H FT
8			M C H FT
9			M C H FT
10			M C H FT

PROSPECT GENERATION SHEET

M = Married   C = Children   H = Home Owner   FT = Full-Time Job

NAME	PHONE	NOTES (CIRCLE APPLICABLE)	
1			M C H FT
2			M C H FT
3			M C H FT
4			M C H FT
5			M C H FT
6			M C H FT
7			M C H FT
8			M C H FT
9			M C H FT
10			M C H FT

FOLLOW UP SHEET

NAME	PHONE	NOTES

DAILY MASSIVE ACTION PLAN

Goals & Affirmations For Day	Time:	Date:

DAILY SCHEDULE	PEOPLE TO CONTACT	THINGS TO DO
6:00am		
7:00am		
8:00am		
9:00am		
10:00am		
11:00am		
12:00 Noon		
1:00pm		
2:00pm		
3:00pm		
4:00pm		

DAILY SCHEDULE	ACTION TAKEN	GOAL	RESULT
5:00pm	PROSPECTS	3-10	
6:00pm	CALLS	20-30	
	INTERVIEWS	1-4	
9:00pm	INVITES	2-5	
	MEETINGS	2-3	
10:00pm	RESULTS CATEGORY	RESULTS	
	RECRUITS		
11:00pm	SALES		
	RESIDUALS		

PROSPECT GENERATION SHEET

M = Married   C = Children   H = Home Owner   FT = Full-Time Job

NAME	PHONE	NOTES (CIRCLE APPLICABLE)
1		M C H FT
2		M C H FT
3		M C H FT
4		M C H FT
5		M C H FT
6		M C H FT
7		M C H FT
8		M C H FT
9		M C H FT
10		M C H FT

PROSPECT GENERATION SHEET

M = Married   C = Children   H = Home Owner   FT = Full-Time Job

NAME	PHONE	NOTES (CIRCLE APPLICABLE)	
1			M C H FT
2			M C H FT
3			M C H FT
4			M C H FT
5			M C H FT
6			M C H FT
7			M C H FT
8			M C H FT
9			M C H FT
10			M C H FT

FOLLOW UP SHEET

NAME	PHONE	NOTES

DAILY MASSIVE ACTION PLAN

Goals & Affirmations For Day	Time:	Date:

DAILY SCHEDULE	PEOPLE TO CONTACT	THINGS TO DO
6:00am		
7:00am		
8:00am		
9:00am		
10:00am		
11:00am		
12:00 Noon		
1:00pm		
2:00pm		
3:00pm		
4:00pm		

DAILY SCHEDULE	ACTION TAKEN	GOAL	RESULT
5:00pm	PROSPECTS	3-10	
6:00pm	CALLS	20-30	
	INTERVIEWS	1-4	
9:00pm	INVITES	2-5	
	MEETINGS	2-3	
10:00pm	RESULTS CATEGORY	RESULTS	
	RECRUITS		
11:00pm	SALES		
	RESIDUALS		

PROSPECT GENERATION SHEET

M = Married   C = Children   H = Home Owner   FT = Full-Time Job

NAME	PHONE	NOTES (CIRCLE APPLICABLE)	
1			M C H FT
2			M C H FT
3			M C H FT
4			M C H FT
5			M C H FT
6			M C H FT
7			M C H FT
8			M C H FT
9			M C H FT
10			M C H FT

PROSPECT GENERATION SHEET

M = Married   C = Children   H = Home Owner   FT = Full-Time Job

NAME	PHONE	NOTES (CIRCLE APPLICABLE)
1		M C H FT
2		M C H FT
3		M C H FT
4		M C H FT
5		M C H FT
6		M C H FT
7		M C H FT
8		M C H FT
9		M C H FT
10		M C H FT

FOLLOW UP SHEET

NAME	PHONE	NOTES

DAILY MASSIVE ACTION PLAN

Goals & Affirmations For Day		Time:		Date:	

DAILY SCHEDULE	PEOPLE TO CONTACT	THINGS TO DO
6:00am		
7:00am		
8:00am		
9:00am		
10:00am		
11:00am		
12:00 Noon		
1:00pm		
2:00pm		
3:00pm		
4:00pm		

	ACTION TAKEN	GOAL	RESULT
5:00pm	PROSPECTS	3-10	
6:00pm	CALLS	20-30	
	INTERVIEWS	1-4	
9:00pm	INVITES	2-5	
	MEETINGS	2-3	

	RESULTS CATEGORY	RESULTS
10:00pm	RECRUITS	
11:00pm	SALES	
	RESIDUALS	

PROSPECT GENERATION SHEET

M = Married   C = Children   H = Home Owner   FT = Full-Time Job

NAME	PHONE	NOTES (CIRCLE APPLICABLE)
1		M C H FT
2		M C H FT
3		M C H FT
4		M C H FT
5		M C H FT
6		M C H FT
7		M C H FT
8		M C H FT
9		M C H FT
10		M C H FT

PROSPECT GENERATION SHEET

M = Married   C = Children   H = Home Owner   FT = Full-Time Job

NAME	PHONE	NOTES (CIRCLE APPLICABLE)	
1			M C H FT
2			M C H FT
3			M C H FT
4			M C H FT
5			M C H FT
6			M C H FT
7			M C H FT
8			M C H FT
9			M C H FT
10			M C H FT

FOLLOW UP SHEET

NAME	PHONE	NOTES

DAILY MASSIVE ACTION PLAN

Goals & Affirmations For Day	Time:	Date:

DAILY SCHEDULE	PEOPLE TO CONTACT	THINGS TO DO
6:00am		
7:00am		
8:00am		
9:00am		
10:00am		
11:00am		
12:00 Noon		
1:00pm		
2:00pm		
3:00pm		
4:00pm		

DAILY SCHEDULE	ACTION TAKEN	GOAL	RESULT
5:00pm	PROSPECTS	3-10	
	CALLS	20-30	
6:00pm	INTERVIEWS	1-4	
	INVITES	2-5	
9:00pm	MEETINGS	2-3	
10:00pm	RESULTS CATEGORY	RESULTS	
	RECRUITS		
11:00pm	SALES		
	RESIDUALS		

PROSPECT GENERATION SHEET

M = Married   C = Children   H = Home Owner   FT = Full-Time Job

NAME	PHONE	NOTES (CIRCLE APPLICABLE)	
1			M C H FT
2			M C H FT
3			M C H FT
4			M C H FT
5			M C H FT
6			M C H FT
7			M C H FT
8			M C H FT
9			M C H FT
10			M C H FT

PROSPECT GENERATION SHEET

M = Married   C = Children   H = Home Owner   FT = Full-Time Job

NAME	PHONE	NOTES (CIRCLE APPLICABLE)	
1			M C H FT
2			M C H FT
3			M C H FT
4			M C H FT
5			M C H FT
6			M C H FT
7			M C H FT
8			M C H FT
9			M C H FT
10			M C H FT

FOLLOW UP SHEET

NAME	PHONE	NOTES

DAILY MASSIVE ACTION PLAN

Goals & Affirmations For Day	Time:	Date:

DAILY SCHEDULE	PEOPLE TO CONTACT	THINGS TO DO
6:00am		
7:00am		
8:00am		
9:00am		
10:00am		
11:00am		
12:00 Noon		
1:00pm		
2:00pm		
3:00pm		
4:00pm		

DAILY SCHEDULE	ACTION TAKEN	GOAL	RESULT
5:00pm	PROSPECTS	3-10	
	CALLS	20-30	
6:00pm	INTERVIEWS	1-4	
	INVITES	2-5	
9:00pm	MEETINGS	2-3	

	RESULTS CATEGORY	RESULTS	
10:00pm	RECRUITS		
11:00pm	SALES		
	RESIDUALS		

PROSPECT GENERATION SHEET

M = Married   C = Children   H = Home Owner   FT = Full-Time Job

NAME	PHONE	NOTES (CIRCLE APPLICABLE)	
1			M C H FT
2			M C H FT
3			M C H FT
4			M C H FT
5			M C H FT
6			M C H FT
7			M C H FT
8			M C H FT
9			M C H FT
10			M C H FT

PROSPECT GENERATION SHEET

M = Married   C = Children   H = Home Owner   FT = Full-Time Job

NAME	PHONE	NOTES (CIRCLE APPLICABLE)
1		M C H FT
2		M C H FT
3		M C H FT
4		M C H FT
5		M C H FT
6		M C H FT
7		M C H FT
8		M C H FT
9		M C H FT
10		M C H FT

FOLLOW UP SHEET

NAME	PHONE	NOTES

DAILY MASSIVE ACTION PLAN

Goals & Affirmations For Day	Time:	Date:

DAILY SCHEDULE	PEOPLE TO CONTACT	THINGS TO DO
6:00am		
7:00am		
8:00am		
9:00am		
10:00am		
11:00am		
12:00 Noon		
1:00pm		
2:00pm		
3:00pm		
4:00pm		

	ACTION TAKEN	GOAL	RESULT
5:00pm	PROSPECTS	3-10	
6:00pm	CALLS	20-30	
	INTERVIEWS	1-4	
9:00pm	INVITES	2-5	
	MEETINGS	2-3	
10:00pm	RESULTS CATEGORY	RESULTS	
	RECRUITS		
11:00pm	SALES		
	RESIDUALS		

PROSPECT GENERATION SHEET

M = Married   C = Children   H = Home Owner   FT = Full-Time Job

NAME	PHONE	NOTES (CIRCLE APPLICABLE)
1		M C H FT
2		M C H FT
3		M C H FT
4		M C H FT
5		M C H FT
6		M C H FT
7		M C H FT
8		M C H FT
9		M C H FT
10		M C H FT

PROSPECT GENERATION SHEET

M = Married C = Children H = Home Owner FT = Full-Time Job

NAME	PHONE	NOTES (CIRCLE APPLICABLE)	
1			M C H FT
2			M C H FT
3			M C H FT
4			M C H FT
5			M C H FT
6			M C H FT
7			M C H FT
8			M C H FT
9			M C H FT
10			M C H FT

FOLLOW UP SHEET

NAME	PHONE	NOTES

TEAM INFO SHEET

Name: _____
DOB: _____
Phone: _____
Email: _____
Address: _____

_____
Spouse: _____
Kids: _____

Name: _____
DOB: _____
Phone: _____
Email: _____
Address: _____

_____
Spouse: _____
Kids: _____

Name: _____
DOB: _____
Phone: _____
Email: _____
Address: _____

_____
Spouse: _____
Kids: _____

Name: _____
DOB: _____
Phone: _____
Email: _____
Address: _____

_____
Spouse: _____
Kids: _____

Name: _____
DOB: _____
Phone: _____
Email: _____
Address: _____

_____
Spouse: _____
Kids: _____

Name: _____
DOB: _____
Phone: _____
Email: _____
Address: _____

_____
Spouse: _____
Kids: _____

Name: _____
DOB: _____
Phone: _____
Email: _____
Address: _____

_____
Spouse: _____
Kids: _____

Name: _____
DOB: _____
Phone: _____
Email: _____
Address: _____

_____
Spouse: _____
Kids: _____

Name: _____
DOB: _____
Phone: _____
Email: _____
Address: _____

_____
Spouse: _____
Kids: _____

Name: _____
DOB: _____
Phone: _____
Email: _____
Address: _____

_____
Spouse: _____
Kids: _____

TEAM INFO SHEET

Name: _____   Name: _____
DOB: _____   DOB: _____
Phone: _____   Phone: _____
Email: _____   Email: _____
Address: _____   Address: _____

_____   _____
Spouse: _____   Spouse: _____
Kids: _____   Kids: _____

Name: _____   Name: _____
DOB: _____   DOB: _____
Phone: _____   Phone: _____
Email: _____   Email: _____
Address: _____   Address: _____

_____   _____
Spouse: _____   Spouse: _____
Kids: _____   Kids: _____

Name: _____   Name: _____
DOB: _____   DOB: _____
Phone: _____   Phone: _____
Email: _____   Email: _____
Address: _____   Address: _____

_____   _____
Spouse: _____   Spouse: _____
Kids: _____   Kids: _____

Name: _____   Name: _____
DOB: _____   DOB: _____
Phone: _____   Phone: _____
Email: _____   Email: _____
Address: _____   Address: _____

_____   _____
Spouse: _____   Spouse: _____
Kids: _____   Kids: _____

Name: _____   Name: _____
DOB: _____   DOB: _____
Phone: _____   Phone: _____
Email: _____   Email: _____
Address: _____   Address: _____

_____   _____
Spouse: _____   Spouse: _____
Kids: _____   Kids: _____